getting to value

author

Quentin Grant McCullough

editor

Diana Cairns

cover design

Wilmie Pretorius

for my boys

Gavin, George and Gareth

contents

professionalise 161

asset of value 196

toolbox 204

navigating the business journey

I have broken up this business journey into seven parts, and it is designed as a checklist for you as an entrepreneur. It guides you through the anticipated future life cycle of your business.

This journey is structured in chapters and explains the process of planning for a new business from your initial idea to the point where you need to decide on what to do with this asset of value you have created.

These chapters contain no magic formula on how to make lots of money quickly, and they contain no new modern theories on business strategy. It is simply a collection of valuable things I have learnt from the people I have worked for and the people who have worked for me, as well as the insights I have gained from books and journals penned by academics, business leaders, economists and politicians. I have always encouraged my employees to look out for better ways to do things, and to listen and learn from everything happening around them. The habit of challenging situations with an open mind and enthusiastically embracing change wherever appropriate is the pathway to developing a successful business.

part 1 - introduction

I introduce myself and explain the reasons for the book. I ask questions about being an entrepreneur and discuss mentorship. Finally, I tell you a personal story about my experience of developing a new product in the life cycle of a business.

part 2 – research

In this section, I talk about the touch-points of a business and the importance of researching a business idea to evaluate its financial viability before developing a business plan.

part 3 - plan

This section emphasises the importance of planning the future of your business. It encourages you to focus on how to achieve your goal, and to think beyond the initial idea.

part 4 - start

Starting a business is no doubt one of the most difficult things you will ever do. In order to assist you with achieving the best possible outcome, I discuss key areas which need attention before you start. At the same time, I encourage entrepreneurs not to discard the mind-set which they started with, and to tackle startup challenges with courage and determination.

part 5 – add value

As the business grows, adding value and innovation should become a way of life to stay ahead of that life cycle curve. We explore possibilities within each of the touch-points.

part 6 – professionalise

Once the business is running well, it is time to prepare the path for it to become an asset of value. This will allow the business to become less dependent on the services of the startup entrepreneurs for its success.

part 7 – asset of value

In this section, we look at some intervention processes to extract personal value from the asset created.

support

In many instances, because a simple graphic could not illustrate a point I was trying to make, I decided to develop some support files. These support files have been created in Microsoft Excel and Adobe PDF which can be downloaded from the BizzBean website. You may modify them to suit your own unique requirements, should you wish to do so. In the first instance, however, they were designed as interactive teaching tools. I hope you find them useful.

Thank you for allowing me to take you on this journey!

part 1

introduction

During the course of this section, I will ask if you to see yourself as an entrepreneur. You will also learn about the importance of mentorship. In order to illustrate how a successful business strategy plays out in real life, I share a personal story with you about a product and how it affected the life cycle of a business.

why the book

My thirty-year career as a professional manager afforded me the opportunity to learn a great deal about the science of business. It set me on the path to running my own consultancy business targeted to assist and advise small, medium and startup businesses.

I began my accounting career as an articled clerk in a small firm of Chartered Accountants based in Johannesburg, South Africa. This provided me with a solid foundation for learning a set of business values which guided me throughout my life. This firm was successfully founded on the basis of a verbal agreement. The partners set and demanded very high standards of work, and they led from the front. They made it clear to all their young articled clerks that they could not afford to make mistakes and had a duty to protect the firm's reputation. Amongst other things, this meant that the staff had to be honest, especially when it came to their most hated duty, which was filling out time sheets. Integrity within the firm was non-negotiable.

I left the auditing profession and moved into commerce. I chose to work for the corporations which I believed shared my acquired value-set, and I chose well. I believe that I added value to the corporations I worked for, but more importantly, I knew that they added value to my career. Along the way, I acquired knowledge and experience, and I eventually decided that it was time for me to change direction again and do things for myself. I decided to start my own business and that is where I started learning all over again. I wanted to advise young entrepreneurs on how to successfully start and manage their own businesses whilst in the process of starting my own business.

It was here that I faced challenges which I had not anticipated. I believed that my knowledge, experience and reputation would get me firmly into the fast lane, but that did not happen. I had no option but to sit down one day, take some time off, and do for myself what I was encouraging my clients to do. I decided that there was no substitute for good planning.

I had developed methodologies, insights and proprietary business tools from years of personal work experience within a broad spectrum of industries, and my good friend Manie Du Preez, an IT professional, suggested that we transfer this intellectual property onto a cloud-based platform. This would allow us to institutionalise the IP and sell it, more affordably, to a wider range of clients, both nationally and internationally.

It was at this point that BizzBean was born.

what is BizzBean?

BizzBean is a company which develops forecasting, budgeting and evaluation software so that entrepreneurs can assess a business scenario and make an informed financial decision.

Quentin G McCullough

are you an entrepreneur?

Are entrepreneurs born or are they nurtured?

I do not know the answer to that, but I do know one thing that most entrepreneurs have in common – they do not have ears! Of course, I am joking, but I do know that when entrepreneurs have an idea, they are unstoppable. Most of the entrepreneurs I have met possess the following characteristics: determination, confidence, energy, high work ethic, impatience, optimism and single-mindedness. They do not sweat the small stuff, which means they often need help with administration issues. More importantly, however, they are not afraid of failure. To them, failure is just another step on the ladder to success. They do not like the term 'yes but' and prefer to hear 'why not?'

This begs the question: Should entrepreneurs have their own businesses?

The answer is: 'not necessarily'.

Entrepreneurs tend to treat the businesses they run as their own. They are motivated by success and like to be rewarded for their efforts. I worked for a very successful South African public company and the CEO won an award for being the 'Best Entrepreneur in the World'. He had a simple philosophy – decentralise operations and reward management for their success with 'top-up' allocations of share options. True entrepreneurs, however, like to manage their own companies and want to control their destinies.

In my opinion, the best entrepreneurs have often had a taste of structured corporate life and have decided to use their acquired knowledge and experience as a springboard for their own success.

Are you an entrepreneur? Read on to find out.

Below, I set out a short 'checklist' of items you should measure yourself against, although it is not a score-card. Only you can decide whether you have what it takes to start your own business, and sometimes you need to heed the words of one of the world's most famous entrepreneurs, Sir Richard Branson, when he says, 'Screw It, Let's Do It'.

acumen

Do you have the skills, attitudes and experience to be successful?

consider:
- I am amenable to new and innovative ideas
- I can foster a culture of innovation
- I am confident my concept is so unique that it stands out from the others
- I am confident my previous work experience will add value
- I am considering the appointment of a mentor
- I am confident that the goals I have set are realistic and achievable
- I can make money for myself
- I understand the importance of finance and record keeping in my business
- I can manage my time well

confidence

Do you have the confidence to be successful?

consider:
- I have self-belief
- I like being independent
- I will get things done
- I will make decisions

- I will solve tough problems
- I will think positively
- I do not concern myself with what others think about me
- I have the courage to try new things
- I will be strong
- I will lead

energy

Do you have the energy to be successful?

consider:

- I have the energy and drive to succeed
- I can work long hours for extended periods of time
- I am in good health and I take care of myself
- I thrive on pressure
- I do not see problems - I see challenges
- I can manage several projects simultaneously
- I do not panic easily – I am calm in crisis situations
- I can cope with stressful situations

determination

Do you have the determination to be successful?

consider:

- I make things happen
- I do not quit
- I work hard
- I will find answers to problems when I do not have solutions
- I set and achieve goals
- I do not avoid difficult situations

lifestyle

Do you have the will to change your lifestyle in order to be successful?

consider:

- I am willing to put my work before social activities

- I am willing to take a reduction in income
- I have the support of my family
- I will be able to maintain a personal and family life while I run my business
- I will be able to sustain my family during the startup phase of my business
- I have considered options in the event of failure, particularly for my family

people skills

Do you have the people skills to be successful?

consider:

- I understand the importance of getting on with people
- I understand the need to hire good people, who relate to my values
- I will ask for and listen to advice
- I understand the need for communication with employees, customers and suppliers
- I can delegate tasks and responsibilities
- I understand the need to trust people

problem solving

Do you have the skills to solve problems and be successful?

consider:

- I will consider new and innovative ways of doing things
- I thrive on challenges
- I find creative solutions to problems
- I thrive on learning new things
- I accept the need for change
- I seek solutions by asking fundamental questions using how? what? when and when not? where and where not? why and why not?

realism

Do you have a realistic view of things to be successful?

consider:

- I understand the need to set realistic goals
- I understand the need to set plans to achieve my goals
- I understand the need to balance enthusiasm with caution
- I understand the need to evaluate results and adjust plans accordingly
- I understand there may be severe consequences in taking uncalculated risks
- I understand that mistakes happen
- I understand my strengths and weaknesses

are you an entrepreneur? – in summary

You have a good chance of succeeding as an entrepreneur if you:

- are innovative and have an inquiring mind
- have confidence in your abilities
- have boundless energy
- have a determined personality
- are prepared to adjust your present lifestyle
- can manage people
- are good at solving problems
- are realistic

learn from someone

I can clearly remember my first day at work.

I started by signing my contract. I was introduced to the Partners and my new colleagues. I attended a short meeting where the Partners spent some time getting to know a little more about me. They outlined the history of the firm and explained to me how seriously they accepted the responsibility of their duties towards their client's shareholders. They talked about how much value they placed on reputation and stressed that the reputation of the firm was a product of the collective behaviour of all the people it employed. Fortunately, I had learnt valuable lessons growing up, and in spite of my youth, I was ready to accept the challenge of upholding my firm's reputation.

My upbringing had equipped me to take my studies seriously, and to open my mind to learning new things. On that first day at work, I learnt another valuable lesson. I was taught to do something for myself by a very wise man, who was assigned to guide me through my audit career. He sat down with me and outlined his approach to adding value to our clients. Simply put, he believed that if we were better informed we could add value to our clients. He made me realise that it was our clients who paid our salaries and that if I wanted to increase my salary, I had to put myself in a position where I could add more value.

This made sense to me, so I started collecting information. I would take a walk around a client's business and get to know the people. I would get to know how their systems worked. I would take copies of documents which I felt were informative and file them in my home-grown filing system. I tried to understand the client's business model and I would make a flow diagram of their supply chain by analysing the profile of their customers and suppliers. I made it my duty to find out who their competitors were. I talked to people within the businesses to see what I could learn from them. Everyone was potentially a source of information. I studied our clients' financials to understand the flow of funds and always tried to ascertain where management could improve the profitability of the business. I subscribed to financial journals and read newspapers and books, and my filing system grew over the years.

a South African challenge

I am a very proud South African. In 1994, I was fortunate to witness the birth of a new democracy in my country. South Africa has always been challenged with a very high number of unemployed people, and while much is being done to address this situation, the problem is likely to prevail for a long time to come. Even if the economic growth rate in the country improves, South Africa will continue to suffer from a lack of suitably qualified and skilled people within the country because not enough people have received the education and training necessary to support the rate of growth required to close this gap.

South Africans, however, do not lack entrepreneurial spirit. One just needs to look at the number of street vendors to see to what lengths people will go to in order to fend for themselves and their families. The South African Government has set up many agencies to address this serious unemployment problem. These agencies provide prospective entrepreneurs with funds to have their business idea captured into a business plan, which can only be done by an approved service provider. They do not necessarily provide funding for the actual businesses, and there are still too many of these startup businesses which fail for one reason or another.

Tim the entrepreneur

I volunteered my services to an agency to provide a mentorship service to young entrepreneurs. After a very exhaustive selection process, I was allocated to a young man whom I will call Tim.

Tim had no money and he had very little education, but he had tons of drive and enthusiasm. He wanted to make a special water heater, which he believed would sell like hot cakes. He based his research on his personal experience and nothing more.

For a very nominal fee, Tim could purchase from this Government agency, a business startup voucher worth a hundred times the face value of his original investment. He could only redeem this voucher at 'approved' service providers. He selected a service provider and he asked them to develop a business plan for his idea. I do not know how long it took them to develop this plan, but Tim very proudly presented this document to me at our first private mentorship session. I was shocked, and Tim saw my reaction.

In my view, there was no substance to Tim's idea, but nevertheless, I decided to invest some time in him and I proposed that I take him through my process of planning his business. His enthusiasm was infectious and I believed he deserved an opportunity. Tim, however, was also impatient and had enormous self-belief. He had a business plan which promised him great wealth almost immediately. My relationship with him did not last long, but I followed his progress from a distance.

With his self-confidence, he convinced a large corporation to back his idea. The South African Government had introduced legislation which required large corporations to spend, amongst other things, a portion of their taxed profits on developing new enterprises, owned or partly owned by 'previously disadvantaged' South Africans.

Tim took advantage of this opportunity, and very soon this corporation fell into the trap of dancing to his tune. They insisted that he attend their mentorship program. The corporation guided him through the re-development of his business plan, and this plan was presented to a bank, which declined the initial funding request. Pressured by Tim, the corporation agreed to fund the production of the required startup asset as a 'grant'. The bank granted a loan facility based on this transaction, and the bank was also required to fund enterprise development projects in terms of legislation.

Tim eventually got his business going, but when the bank funding arrived, he was overwhelmed by the sight of a brand-new BMW motor vehicle parked in the showroom at the local dealership, and he purchased it.

This acquisition did not, however, form part of his business plan, and within a year, Tim had to sell the BMW.

Tim's business failed.

what went wrong?

The South African Government set up huge and costly infrastructures to support entrepreneurship. Who really benefitted from this situation? It appears that the service provider who was chosen to develop the original business plan benefitted, and so did the people who were employed by the government agency to distribute this money. The corporation that took on Tim's project and the bank that provided finance could claim points on their score-card. Money was spent in the economy, not by supporting Tim to develop his own startup asset, but by supplying 'mentoring money' to a company that was already well established. The idea of entrepreneurship was replaced with 'learnerships'. The result was government investing in existing leadership rather than promoting new leadership.

Tim's case is not unique. There are thousands of similar examples. The country wasted a lot of money on him and this process contributed to the statistic that ninety percent of new businesses fail within a very short time after being started up.

The Government should focus on creating an environment which stimulates economic activity, rather than subsidising business plans for 'wannabe' entrepreneurs. Developing thousands of small businesses with no economic activity is simply a waste of money.

Tim had passion and enthusiasm, but he was also very impatient and stubborn. He had been given an opportunity but refused to learn. The world is changing rapidly, and besides the idea, Tim needed to know how to go about starting his new business. He needed to think about how he would fund his business, how he would administer it, what laws he needed to adhere to, what skills he needed to develop and grow his business, and most importantly, he needed to gain access to key markets to sell his products.

Was he prepared to run a business? In my opinion: no! Should he have been given an opportunity? In my opinion: yes!

the value of mentorship

Tim's business idea was doomed without money. Tim had no money, so he successfully convinced a few large corporations to invest in his idea. After the business was started, he was left to his own devices and he bought a BMW, which was not in the plan.

Let us investigate another scenario.

Tim approached a professional business mentorship agency. The agency would, in principle, take him through a structured process to achieve his objectives.

assess the jockey and the horse

The agency would evaluate Tim's idea in terms of its viability. It would also assess his personal background and his leadership abilities. This process will eliminate the waste of time and money in preparing expensive business and financial plans, which may not be favourably considered. Tim would be expected to pay for this service. By doing so, he demonstrates his personal commitment to the project.

obtain a mentorship sponsor

Once accepted, Tim would sign a performance agreement with the mentorship agency. Failure on his part to perform in terms of this agreement would result in him losing his sponsorship and he will be kicked off the program. The mentorship agency may also choose to invest in Tim's business or find a suitable investment partner for him.

structured program of action

Tim would attend a structured program, whereby the mentorship agency would assist him with the development of his business strategy and starting his business. At the same time, he would also attend skills training sessions, which are synchronised to accommodate his mentorship meetings. He would have access to qualified guidance counsellors, who will assist him to develop his personal goals and instil self-confidence to make and implement decisions that affect his business.

accounting and administration

The mentorship agency will be staffed with professional accounting people, who will keep his books up-to-date and attend to all other administration functions within his business. Tim would meet with this team on a regular basis to discuss his financial results. During this process, he would learn to read and interpret his financial statements.

possible outcome

I am not sure whether this process is totally fool-proof. There is always a chance that Tim's business may also have failed by following this formula. However, I personally believe there would have been more chance of success. Tim would have learned a lot about business from professional managers. He would have learned that business is not only about that great idea he woke up with one morning. He would not have needed to worry about the administration aspects of the business, which would have allowed him more time to generate that much needed startup revenue. He would learn that acquiring new revenue may require further investment within his business. He would not have bought the BMW. Tim would have learned how to work with people and how to be a better leader. He may have found that, even though he was the boss, he had responsibilities to other stakeholders. He may have learned how to better direct those wonderful qualities he possessed – a sense of urgency and a great deal of enthusiasm.

Tim brought about his own failure. He failed to learn from people with knowledge and experience.

Perhaps I was more fortunate to have been taught from a young age to absorb the knowledge handed to me by my parents and mentors. Little did I know how much this would be to my advantage when I listened to the advice of my first mentor at the beginning of my career.

learn from someone - in summary

Make it your duty to learn from successful business leaders.

I received some very sound advice from a senior mining executive. He suggested to me that I should never work for anybody unless they were a lot smarter than I am. Furthermore, he suggested that I should never hire anyone to work directly for me unless they were also a lot smarter than I am.

Never waste an opportunity to learn something new. Attend as many training and development programs as are offered to you and do not complete the programs in order to fill your wall with certificates – rather do them to implement the outcome of your acquired knowledge.

Track the progress of successful leaders. Read their autobiographies. Get to know them personally if you can. Keep a little black book.

Do not believe you can do it by yourself.

a journey

'Everything that is possible has been invented'.

This statement was made by Charles Holland Duell (April 13, 1850 – January 29, 1920). He was the commissioner of the United States Patent and Trademark Office from 1898 to 1901, and later became a United States federal judge.

How incorrect was this statement?

You are in the very important research phase of setting up your business and you are about to start your journey. I introduce you to the generally accepted theory that all products and businesses have a life cycle. In this fast and ever-changing world that we live in, you must plan to change. If you do not change, some new 'kid on the block' may ruin your journey.

the business and product life cycle

One day I was chatting to a few young entrepreneurs and they marvelled at what I had personally witnessed during my lifetime.

I was a young boy when the first human was launched into space, and I listened to that broadcast on an FM transistor radio. Over a decade later, I listened to the broadcast of the first human being landing on the Moon, also on an FM transistor radio. A few years later, I was able to enjoy my favourite music programme broadcasting from that same FM radio, in stereo. My dad took me to see the first passenger jetliner, the Comet, arrive in South Africa. In 1985, I bought my first personal computer and I was envied by my peers because it had 64kbs of memory, a hard disk of 10mb and a colour screen. I was in awe because I could use a fax machine in 1986. In 1994, I used a cellular phone for the first time, and very soon after that, I had access to the Internet, through a 9800-baud dialup modem. I have been lucky enough to experience the invention of many things which I take for granted today.

As the discussion broadened, one youngster made a statement suggesting that too much money was being wasted on space adventures, and his comment, of course, was related to philanthropic issues. He believed that more money should be diverted towards health care research. I simply said to him 'somebody up there is probably planning the downfall of your new businesses'. He looked at me with a blank stare on his face, so we explored some examples.

My father's generation saw the invention of television, while I assumed that it had always been around. My generation saw the invention of a fax machine, but my grandchildren will probably never use one. I used to buy a map book on a regular basis but today's motorist gets directions to his friends, clients or hotels from maps freely available on the internet or uses a GPS system, either on his mobile phone or installed in his motor vehicle.

Good business people innovate all the time to gain a competitive advantage. An entertaining read to illustrate this philosophy is Sir Richard Branson's autobiography, 'Losing my Virginity'.

Whatever you are planning to do, plan to change and plan to add value.

NGK Spark Plugs – South Africa

I was fortunate to have a very close working relationship with the NGK Spark Plug Co, a Japanese Spark Plug manufacturer. I was appointed to manage a company which held the licence to manufacture these high-quality spark plugs in South Africa. At the time, the company was not in good shape and the NGK brand struggled with a very low share of the market.

My enthusiasm to tackle this challenge was unlimited and very soon I began shaping my strategy for the future of this brand.

My enthusiasm, however, was tempered by a 'Samurai Warrior'. This man was the resident NGK Spark Plug Co factory representative, a Japanese man, who had oversight over issues such as quality and brand reputation. He wanted to be involved in my planning process and gave me some insights into his thought process. I listened to him and soon realised that he had successfully changed the fortunes of a company before. I needed to make changes to the company in a hurry, but he needed to change things within the NGK brand for the long term. I realised I was in for a very frustrating challenge. I discussed my frustration with the chairman of my holding company. He encouraged me to put my pride in my pocket and work with this Japanese man. 'The Japanese' he said, 'take a long-term view of situations and achieve their goals by implementing small but well-planned activities'.

I reluctantly decided to work with him and see how we could both achieve our objectives. I remember him saying to me: 'A good plan, in the hands of a good manager, will always get the attention of an enlightened investor'. Together we started a process which resulted in the NGK Spark Plug brand increasing its market share four-fold over a relatively short period in South Africa. The fortunes of the company changed dramatically. Its dominant position in South Africa remains unchallenged. The South African operation contributed to the NGK Spark Plug Co achieving a long-term objective. That objective was never made public, and when it was achieved, they were humble in their success.

Many years later my youngest son, Gareth, asked me whether what we did at NGK Spark Plugs had any reference to what he was learning at university at the time – he was referring to a business and product life cycle. I looked at the curve and I recalled our efforts. There were similarities, I recalled, but I realised that there was one big difference – most people need to learn how to plan, while the Japanese people do it instinctively. I had no reason to believe that my 'Samurai

Warrior' was taking me through a well-researched theory on how to plan - I assumed it was just the Japanese way of doing things. Let us have a look at what we did and how our actions can be 'blocked' into the headings ascribed to the famous 'J' curve.

the idea - identifying the opportunity

We knew we had problems. We were losing money. Our quality was poor. We did not have a distribution strategy and we had management issues. We knew we had to do something different to get out of our negative situation. Just sorting out these issues was not good enough for our Samurai Warrior. He encouraged us to look beyond the problems. We started looking at each of the components in our business, such as products, customers, suppliers, employees, infrastructure and systems. I refer to these elements as business touch-points. We evaluated each of these touch-points objectively and compared them to those of our competitors. We made a list of the 'burning issues' we had to address.

We found ourselves doing two things: identifying problems and brainstorming solutions at the same time. It became an interactive process. In the beginning, I thought it would take forever, but we got through the process quickly.

You may get the impression that we were writing a huge planning document, which detailed every little decision and action step required to implement a big overall plan. Yes, I captured the details in a well written document, but it was never published. What in fact happened was that our management team began to form. This process also gave me an opportunity to evaluate each team member. I made changes to the team when I realised that certain members did not have the ability to execute their portion of the plan. The enthusiasm within the team became infectious. Members realised how important is was to buy into a common vision, and furthermore, they realised how the inefficiencies of one team member affected the overall performance of the team. Lots of little things started happening within the business, and they happened because people became involved in solving problems. There was no need to refer to a list of things written down in an overall plan. People became aware of the problems and accepted responsibility to initiate and implement change within the business.

One day, our technical manager presented me with a spark plug, which had a grooved centre core. He talked about its technical qualities and outlined the benefits which we could offer by selling this spark plug to our customers. In all honesty, I did not see a spark plug – I saw an opportunity. My mind raced with excitement and I remember telling my technical manager to keep our discussion secret. Soon after that I met with my Samurai Warrior and shared my excitement at the opportunity that this product could add to our business. Without emotion, he looked at me and said: 'It is a very good product, but it may not necessarily work in your region. Go and find out if you have a market – then we will help you'. It was like pouring a bucket of cold water over my head. I just wanted action. Not being a technical person, I did not appreciate that the performance of these spark plugs could be affected by, amongst other things, climate conditions and the quality of petroleum products distributed in South Africa at the time. I immediately called a meeting of my team and announced my plan to research the idea, stressing to them that it was to remain a secret at all costs. They supported my decision.

research

I took responsibility for the research project. I must admit I was very frustrated at the time. My Samurai Warrior invited me to travel to many NGK research facilities located in Europe and Japan. I learnt why it was so important to do research. Again, I became very aware of how cautious the Japanese were when it came to the introduction of new products. I witnessed some research projects where I saw how NGK Spark Plug Co worked with their customers to develop products.

I also learnt to embrace the Japanese mind-set towards research, which is to spend money in order to make more money in the long run, and also to spend money to avoid wasting money. Plans are only implemented when there is some guarantee of success.

We appointed an independent scientific research laboratory to evaluate the performance of these spark plugs and compare these results to our own products and those of our competitors. At the same time, we ran our own tests and involved strategic customers in these tests. We commissioned our advertising agency to work with the research laboratory on developing the 'positioning strategy'.

When the initial research project returned very favourable results, we set the planning process in motion.

plan

Although I had captured the details of the research project into a well written document, it was never published. However, we now had an opportunity to take the idea of a grooved spark plug and make it into a business. Unlike the technical guys, I had a vision that this spark plug could re-launch the company and get it back onto a path of sustained profitability.

By this stage, I had realised that we had transformed the management style of our company. No longer did the bosses sit in their offices and make decisions. Decisions were now being made with input from everyone in the company. Our people were being consulted and we realised that this process appeared to be slower, but when it came to the implementation of decisions there was a significant saving in time and money. I decided to call a meeting of the whole company and share my vision for the grooved spark plug with them. They were aware of the problems which we faced in returning the company to a profitable position, and they knew that the company's failure would have serious consequences.

I outlined my plans and challenged all my employees to assist me in making a dream come true. I asked only one thing of them: To keep the project a secret.

The planning process began and I took responsibility for the project. We would launch the new product in five months.

We had now become conditioned to planning for our future. We had started by getting the fundamentals of our business in order, and it was time to introduce a new idea into the business with a view to long-term growth of the company. This required more interactive planning. The new grooved spark plug had to be integrated into our existing business processes and this required a mind-set change. The new product we offered improved fuel consumption and would last longer but its manufacturing cost was only marginally higher than that of a standard spark plug. If we were successful with this new spark plug, we could be the losers in the long-term. We would be making and selling fewer spark plugs in the future. On my visits to the NGK research centres, I was exposed to many new innovations in spark plug technology and it became very clear to me that I would have to work very hard to increase the selling price of our spark plugs into the future. Engine manufacturers demanded longer lasting spark plugs because they were under pressure to reduce the cost of servicing a vehicle. A spark plug would last 100,000 kilometres instead of every 15,000 kilometres. I was faced with a real dilemma. The components that make up a spark plug would cost more but the cost to assemble a spark plug would not rise if there were no reductions in production volumes. We had a big investment in infrastructure and indeed we also employed many people, which is an important factor in South Africa. We realised that we had to develop a strategy which would allow us to increase our market share and at the same time increase the selling value of our products into the future.

I sat down and crunched the numbers. I worked out what we needed to do. Again, we called all our people together, and shared the challenges we faced going forward.

I remember the meeting we held to discuss the launch date. I had no say in the date of our launch, and there was no science behind their decision. South Africans are sports crazy and my production people decided that we should launch our television campaign on the day of the Currie Cup Rugby Final. We had five months to plan.

We set up a large planning board in our board room. We appointed a small planning team to work out what needed to be done by whom and by when. We reviewed, argued and came to an agreement on the action plan. We assigned responsibility and met regularly to review progress. It was a very exciting period, but it was also extremely stressful. I remember looking at the cash flow, which was going according to plan, but it was all negative.

We had five months to achieve the following: commission a new manufacturing and assembly line; test our production processes; build a 'launch inventory stockpile'; develop an advertising and marketing plan; review and change our distribution strategy; and upgrade our billing systems.

start

The last month of the project plan called for a great deal of interaction with our customers. Our advertising and communication programs were developed. We started our program in our biggest market, Johannesburg. We invited our distributors and their customers to a lavish launch at which we recognised our employees as guests of honour. This surprised all my employees because I always reminded them that the customer paid their salaries. This move bought us incredible loyalty from our employees, something which would last certainly until the day I moved on from the company. Our customers were also overcome with respect for our decision and it made them regard us in a new light.

The launch programs to introduce our new product to potential consumers around the country were an enormous success, and we achieved our objective. We convinced our distributors and their customers to take in stock to meet the expected demand.

Our television commercial featured in a prime-time slot during the Saturday Currie Cup Rugby Final, and it proved to be an outstanding success. On the Monday following the TV launch, I remember likening the trading conditions in our small sales office to that of the Johannesburg Stock Exchange.

Our key distributors and our employees honoured my secrecy request. Our competitors were caught off-guard. They had a month to react but chose to ignore us. The cash started streaming in and very soon we recouped our 'new venture' investment.

add value

Fortunately, we had planned very well. A few small launch problems which we encountered were dealt with expeditiously. We had, however, woken up an angry lion. We expected a reaction but had no idea what could be thrown at us. In our planning phase, we held several sessions on a 'possible competitor reaction'. We had developed several alternative plans to counter various anticipated responses. We were determined to work on our long-term strategy to increase our market share while increasing selling prices at the same time. A decision was made to adopt an offensive strategy. Spark plugs were traditionally used by motor supplier distributors as 'loss leader' products. The practice of using our products for this purpose was frustrating to us and no doubt to our competitors as well. We worked hard to manufacture and market quality products and our customers had no regard or respect for our values. We deliberately reduced the number of distributors in the effort to improve the communication of our strategy and encourage our distributors to add value to their business by distributing our products. At the same time, however, we had to be extremely careful not to contravene any competition rules.

We now had cash and we decided to re-invest it in achieving our growth strategy. We realised we could not afford to sit back and bask in the glory of our strike-back launch. We continually introduced innovative advertising and promotional campaigns and sponsored motorsport activities to align our brand success. We introduced an extremely effective customer relationship marketing program, which allowed us to keep in touch with the requirements of our customers, and through this mechanism we became aware of competitor activities and continued to invest in our business systems, including quality processes.

Over the next few years we continued to grow our sales, increase our market share and realised prices and we became an extremely profitable business. Our efforts were rewarded with numerous supplier recognition awards.

All of these activities had been planned.

professionalise

I do recall being approached by members of my team with a request to 'slow down'. I became too driven with my mind-set of continual improvement. I did not appreciate that I may have caused some unnecessary stress within the organisation.

Many years later, a young woman in the accounts department challenged me on my attitude towards continual improvement. She believed that we may have departed from our planned strategy to become more professional – she argued that we were obsessed with innovation and that some of our initiatives may have been less effective because we had not allowed sufficient time to bed them down. During the debate, I realised that she had mustered a fair amount of support within the organisation.

It was a good lesson for me. I had become obsessed with growth and innovation at the expense of professionalising our business. I realised I may have forgotten the lessons I learned from my Samurai Warrior. I remembered the words of my chairman, 'The Japanese', he said: 'take a long-term view on situations and achieve goals by implementing small but well-planned activities'.

I realised that we had successfully instilled the concept of planning into our company and the people believed we were successful because we followed strict guidelines. I realised, quite by accident, that we had developed our core values, but had not formalised them. That process came much later and we were lucky in that we had developed our core values as a team.

asset of value

'How did this section affect you, Dad?' This was the question asked by my youngest son, Gareth, referring to the section on innovation and decline.

I looked at the curve again and said, 'We did that first because we knew there was value'. We had our backs to the wall. We had to do something to save our company. We fixed the problems within our company and at the same time we introduced innovations, in terms of products and systems, to achieve our planned objectives.

'So, my boy', I said, 'now you understand why it's called a cycle'. I continued, 'our objective was to always put ourselves ahead of the curve'.

a journey - in summary

I demonstrated how I applied the product and business life cycle concept to the development of a new product – unwittingly, of course.

Your business will always be under threat from competitors and you will always face challenges, but you need to stay ahead of the curve.

part 2

research

We now understand that products are subject to a life cycle and there is a need to constantly add value through innovation to extend their lives. We will discuss adding value at a later stage but before that we need to understand the fundamentals of a business – I call them the touch-points. There are seven touch-points: products, customers, suppliers, employees, infrastructure, systems and a leader. A business will become more efficient when these touch-points operate in unison. It is necessary, therefore, to understand more about them and to optimise value from each of them.

touch-points

Now, let us explore each touch-point in some detail. Before that, however, I would like to make a general comment about 'impressions'.

I am very aware of the 'first impressions' I get when I deal with a supplier or a client. I look at the presentation of the facility. I look at the state of the assets they own and I feel the mood of the employees within the business. I do not judge the business on how modern its facility is – rather on how clean and efficient it is. I do not judge a business on newness of their delivery vehicles - I judge the business on how well they look after their existing 'old' vehicles. I do not judge a business on the good looks of its employees – rather, I judge the business on the efficient and friendly way I am attended to. First impressions count. It is therefore essential to focus on each touch-point of the business.

products

There is no business unless there is a product. The product may be something you have invented; it may be something you re-sell on behalf of a distributor; or it may be a service or skill, which you are uniquely qualified to offer. Products solve customers' problems. Therefore, this asset should be protected and enhanced to optimise value for your business.

If you have invented something unique, make sure you consult a patent attorney to protect your asset against unscrupulous competitors, who will steal and copy your idea and nullify all your hard work in developing your invention. Think about how and who may distribute your products. How can you withdraw distribution rights if a distributor does not perform to agreed expectations? If you re-sell products and services on behalf of a distributor, have you negotiated an equitable agreement with that distributor; do you have a territory agreement; do you have a fair price compared to other re-sellers; do you have a return clause covering defects. There are many issues you need to think about when you negotiate a re-seller agreement. If you have a unique service, which you offer, how do you protect your intellectual property?

Consult and obtain advice from a commercial lawyer on these issues. It is cheaper to obtain this advice before you commence trading than to find out that you are the subject of a misunderstanding, which may cost you a lot more money in the long-run. Remember, these products are assets on which you expect to earn a return, which is linked to your livelihood and that needs protection.

When I evaluate a business, I study the contribution it derives from the products it sells. I evaluate this in terms of unit sales, revenue contribution, gross profit contribution and the cost to distribute the products.

Business managers are very often surprised when they are presented with the results. Very often they are not even aware of these dynamics. I believe that you should introduce systems, early in the establishment of your business, to measure these dynamics. You will be in a good position to analyse opportunities and risks presented by this data. For example: is your business too dependent on one or two products for revenue or gross profit contribution? Data allows you to assess these risks and develop strategies to counter them.

customers

As with a product, you also do not have a business unless you have a customer. In the same way you protect your products, your customers are also an asset and, therefore, you also need to know a lot about them. For the same reason, you may be concerned that your business is too dependent on one or two products for revenue or gross profit contribution, and you may have similar concerns about your customer profile. Is your business too dependent on too few customers? Design and build your systems so that you can evaluate this data. Do this regularly. You do not want to discover that a customer purchased enough from you once in six months and became your top customer – why did they not purchase from you after that?

I have told you how important, I believe it is, to evaluate the performance of your products. Now you need to map that product data against that of your customers. With this information, you will find out if your top customer only buys low margin items. You can work out what costs your business incurs, such as delivery and finance charges, to service that top customer? If you 'do the numbers', you might well discover that this top customer is actually your worst customer.

This type of data presents you, as the business manager, with valuable analysis on your customers and allows you to develop strategies to optimise contributions from your customers and improve profitability.

suppliers

Depending on the type of business, your suppliers may also form an integral part of your supply chain. The profitability of your business can be affected positively or negatively by their performance.

While it may be in the best interest of your business to have a broad spread of customers, it may be more cost effective to have a smaller spread of suppliers. The cost of raising purchase orders and maintaining a large supplier database must be evaluated against many factors, including product costs, quality issues and delivery lead times. Another important dynamic to consider, is the possibility of 'overcharging' resulting from a friendship or favouritism towards a specific supplier. I have seen how operational management can ignore a central procurement system to obtain items, arguing that the central system was inefficient. It may have been, but further investigation revealed that the operational management were being 'rewarded' by suppliers to procure goods from them. I encourage business owners to work hard to gain the loyalty of their customers, and at the same time, I remind them that they should extend the same courtesy to their suppliers. You, as a customer, need to monitor all aspects of supply transactions, just as your customers will monitor supply transactions between their business and yours to justify that loyalty value.

You may want to consider adding various other metrics to evaluate the performance of your suppliers. For example, you may want to measure how consistently your suppliers achieve their actual supply date times as compared to required dates. This measurement may also consider quantity and quality issues.

Once again it may be prudent for you to consult and obtain advice from a commercial lawyer on these issues.

employees

You do not have a business unless you have products and customers. The value of your business will, however, be very reliant on the type of people employed. I always remind employees that it is the customer that pays their salary and I hasten to tell them that it is their actions which may determine the success of the business and consequently their own earnings. The right people in your business have the potential to add real value to it. Just as you work hard to keep your good customers, you need to do the same with good employees. Unfortunately, your wage bill will be one of your biggest costs, and you as the business owner must ensure that you get a return on your investment. Hiring the 'wrong' person will add costs to your business in many ways. Their non-committed attitude, for example, may cost you an important customer.

The most effective way to lighten this cost to your business is to employ the right people in the first place. This is one of the most difficult tasks an entrepreneur will be called upon to do. Employees should be considered the most important asset in your business. On the other hand, their negative attitude will place extra weight on your company's ability to earn profits. I have yet to hear of any organisation that is perfect with their hiring policies. We all make mistakes in this area. Those companies that achieve superior results in this area, however, place a very high value on their employees and when hiring them, know that they, amongst other things, must embrace the company values. It is essential to know what you expect from your employees and to ensure that they understand what you expect from them. Invest in the development of your employees to keep them, but at the same time, act quickly to remove underperforming employees. Poor performing employees add weight to your business and adversely affect profitability.

I always take the view that one must look at issues from a broad perspective first and then focus on the areas which weigh down performance. We will look at some of the measurement methods covering employee productivity and cost efficiency in a later chapter.

infrastructure

Infrastructure includes the assets within your business from which you derive income, such as buildings, vehicles, plant and equipment, furniture and fittings, computer equipment and so on. These assets may be owned or leased.

It is difficult to understand how many companies spend a lot of money buying or leasing these assets but do not look after them. The lack of routine maintenance can cause down-the-line production stoppages, which may well be costlier in terms of lost revenue than the cost of maintenance. Caring for these assets will go a long way to extend their lifespan and improve productivity. It will also add value to the business, and this additional equity must be measured. Systems, however, must be in place to measure the efficiency of these assets, either at their original cost value or their replacement value. For example; the operating costs, including maintenance of an item, may be greater than the cost of the finance and operating costs of a new replacement item; the property you trade from may not yield the turnover per square or cubic metre you could achieve from a perceivably more expensive property. Very often, perceived cost is the benchmark for acquiring an asset.

systems

In my experience, systems are the last thing that are considered when starting a project or a new business. In fact, very often, entrepreneurs pack up all their documents such as invoices, expense vouchers and bank statements into a shoebox and send the box to their accountant or auditor once a year. Alternatively, they might suddenly search for these documents when a set of accounts needs to be prepared for their funder or the tax authorities. Later in this book, I talk about the importance of keeping books of account up-to-date. Right now, I am more concerned about the attributes of all the various business systems you may choose to use. I am very mindful that in the initial stages of a business, cost control is of utmost importance and one cannot invest in all the 'bells and whistles' – as the saying goes; you don't need a battleship to sink a rowboat. Having said that, I believe it is still very important to think about the purpose of having systems within the business and the attributes of a good system.

There are two important reasons to set up good systems within a business. Firstly, one needs to obtain information quickly. This allows the business owner to evaluate situations on the turn and make decisions accordingly. Problems can be addressed immediately, thus avoiding unnecessary waste of money, and conversely, one can take advantage of opportunities which may arise. Secondly, there is the issue of governance – it is necessary to maintain an accurate record of the assets and liabilities of your business.

leader

In the book I refer to the owner as the 'leader'.

The key objective of business leaders is to create an asset of value, which will sustain them while they are working in their businesses and beyond. Leaders, therefore, have the most profound effect on a business and, of course, the other touch-points discussed above.

Leaders, either as a sole person or in a partnership, stand to lose the most should the business fail, and they should stand to gain the most if it succeeds. Risk should be rewarded.

As a leader, the most important duty is to separate your personal goals from those of the business. An old, but important saying is, 'work on the business'. That does not mean that owners must divorce themselves from working in the business. A business owner must be part of the leadership team to set clear goals for the business and initiate plans to achieve those goals. When working in the business, treat yourself as an employee and pay yourself your worth. More importantly, put systems in place to measure and achieve those goals so that the business is sustainable in the absence of you, the leader.

touch-points - in summary

This book aims to guide you on how to develop a new business and to create your asset of value. There are seven fundamental touch-points, which are:

- products
- customers
- suppliers
- employees
- infrastructure
- systems
- leader

will it work?

You know what you want to do and you are all fired up and ready to start your business.

Stop!

do some high-level research first

Before you embark on the next steps, do some basic research first to determine the viability of your product. You also need to find out about the cultural, environmental, legal, political, social and technological issues, which may affect its viability. Will your product offend a cultural group within your market? Environmental issues must be investigated in detail. Find out if you must subject your product to an expensive environmental study. Will your product require a great deal of energy to produce it and what type of energy will be required? Find out what laws or pending laws may impact the launch of your product in any way. Is the political climate stable in the area you intend launching your product? How will decisions of government affect the disposable income of your potential market? You need to find out how changing technology may affect your product.

Market research forms the basis on which the identified opportunity is evaluated. Research establishes the characteristics of the market in which you wish to position your product or service. It also exposes you to the competitor elements within the market. Data acquired through research will be useful in the development of your marketing strategy.

There are two kinds of market research.

primary research

Primary Research is the gathering of specific information, which would provide you with data which is either quantitative or qualitative, in order to make decisions about your project. You could do this research yourself or you could outsource it to professional market research organisations. This research will come in different forms, such as counts, surveys and focus-groups.

download: market share calculator
This Microsoft Excel spreadsheet is designed as an interactive teaching tool. It is designed as a check point to compare forecasted sales against the actual market demographic. The calculator consists of five elements: total market size, primary demographics, secondary demographics, target market and competitors' share. It is designed as a reality check for sales forecasts.

secondary research

Secondary Research is information which you can obtain from public sources such as industry profiles, trade journals, newspapers, magazines, census data, and demographic profiles.

While I advocate the need to research issues around your new product or new project, I am also very mindful of the fact that you can research a project to death. You, by nature, are eager to get on with your business, while professional research houses may have their own interests at heart, causing the project to take longer than necessary. You need to strike a balance, and to do this, you need to know exactly what it is that your research project will establish. Prepare an analysis of your situation and carefully define your opportunity, including the facts you wish to research, such as quantities, industry trends, fashion, change drivers, demographics and psychographics. Plan the implementation phase of the research project carefully and keep yourself involved all the time – this is your best chance to learn about the acceptance of your product and your target markets. Do not be part of the research team, because you also need to maintain your objectivity.

The process of conducting the research is important, but the analysis and interpretation phase is more important. Again, you need to maintain your objectivity. Be careful not to challenge the research, simply because of your personal perceptions.

Use this information to adapt your products and markets and utilise the data to develop your marketing plan and the launch of your product.

You may believe that all the work you do before you start your project is in fact research. It is, and you will be so much better off for it because you have done it thoroughly.

will it work? - in summary

> 'There is never enough time to do it right, but there is
> always time to do it right again'.

I do not know where I learned that, but I always checked myself with these words when my enthusiasm to tackle a project got the better of me.

Do your research first and do it well.

financial viability

adding some science to your business

Martha ran a small laundry business. When I met her, she was in a state of distress - her business was not generating cash and her books of account were in a bit of a mess. I spent a few hours with her and assisted her to understand some basic costing calculations within her business. She burst into tears because for the first time she could understand a few of the basic costing problems she faced. She had a great idea and solicited business based on her understanding of the costs within her business. She gave her customers good service, but they were smarter than she was - her prices were too low. Fortunately, Martha could re-negotiate prices with some of her customers and now she continues to run a thriving laundry business. Her problem stemmed from the fact that she did not understand the dynamics of her production costs. She started her business without knowing the key fundamentals. Her reference point was estimates she compiled on the 'back of a cigarette box'.

Martha is not alone. Many entrepreneurs start their businesses without knowing and understanding the fundamental dynamics of their business. Very often, when evaluating their business idea, they are guided by an accountant or a consultant who uses their own electronic spreadsheet as a financial model. The business gets started and its financial chart of accounts has very little resemblance to the original model, and very often the financial reports do not focus on critical measurement issues. Why should there be differences? A key objective of your business idea is about maximising your financial opportunity.

Should the success of a business be measured by the amount of money it makes, or should it be measured by the quality of the profits it produces?

The answer is both.

When entrepreneurs start their businesses, their natural focus is to drive sales and revenue but in the process, they sometimes forget about measuring the quality of their earnings. There is an old saying which says: 'turnover is vanity, profits are sanity and cash flow is reality'. Of course, no one wants to destroy entrepreneurial enthusiasm, but some warning signs are necessary. Too many businesses fail shortly after they are started and it is not necessarily because of the business idea, but more often because of poor financial management of the business.

Let us investigate five areas in a business, where with some focus, the quality of earnings can be improved.

trading

When we refer to the 'vanity and sanity' of turnover, we are calculating what gross profit is earned and at what margin? Gross profit should be the amount of money earned that is sufficient to exceed the overhead expenses in the business to make a net operating profit. So, let us assume that a business has a monthly overhead expense bill of $100,000 per month:

- a gross profit margin of 20.00% would require a monthly turnover of $500,000 to cover overheads by a factor of 4.00. Formula: 100.00% / 20.00% = 4.00.
- a gross profit margin of 30.00% would require a monthly turnover of $333,333 to cover overheads by a factor of 3.33. Formula: 100.00% / 33.33% = 3.33.

Higher margins make overhead recovery easier. Of course, that assumes that a business can achieve higher margins. Increased margins generally tend to reduce sales volumes while lower margins increase sales volumes. Businesses need to consider the trading environment and tweak the dynamics to achieve an acceptable balance on earnings quality. The product and customer mix are important considerations and the leader needs to consider the following:

- do all products contribute to their full potential?

- will discontinuing low margin earning products have a detrimental effect on the business?
- do all customers contribute positively to the business?
- will closing low margin customer accounts have a detrimental effect on the business?

There is no right or wrong answer to these questions. The solution is to carefully measure the contribution of each product to each customer and ensure that the aggregate result is an efficient gross profit contribution to the business.

download: contribution mix
This Microsoft Excel spreadsheet is designed as an interactive teaching tool. It allows the creation of various product mix scenarios and demonstrates how changes to unit sales volumes, unit selling prices and unit cost prices will affect the aggregate gross profit contribution in a business.

expenses

The difference between gross profit and net operating profit in a business is its operating expenses. Lower expenses obviously reduce pressure on gross profit margins and improve the opportunity to optimise net operating profits. There are two types of expenses: fixed and variable. Fixed expenses are generally those which are predictable in nature, for example, rent and salaries. Variable expenses are those which generally occur in proportion to turnover levels. Lower turnover, in theory, would therefore result in lower variable expenses. As a strategy, business owners should seek out ways to convert as many fixed expenses as possible to those of a variable nature. This strategy has the effect of protecting net operating profit to some extent when turnover is adversely affected for any reason. Conversely, the benefactors of variable expenses, for example salespeople, will benefit when turnover rises. These benefactors will then be motivated to drive turnover at an optimum gross profit margin. Reducing the dependence on fixed expenses can be measured by calculating the breakeven point.

download: breakeven calculator

This Microsoft Excel spreadsheet is designed as an interactive teaching tool. It teaches how to calculate the breakeven point in a trading business. It provides opportunities to simulate 'what if' situations.

taxed profits

To achieve profits, businesses need to borrow money to finance either fixed assets or working capital requirements. Borrowing costs money in the form of interest and once the interest is deducted from the net operating profits, the taxman wants his share. There is very little one can do about paying tax, except to ensure that all legally allowable deductions are processed. When it comes to borrowing money, business owners have some options besides hard bargaining to reduce the rate of interest charged. Borrowings options include the following key instruments:

- term loans – term loans are usually raised to finance startup ventures or projects which are projected to generate sustainable cash flows before the term loan is paid up
- overdrafts - overdrafts are put in place to finance fluctuations in working capital requirements such as inventory and receivables

A key ratio in measuring the affordability of interest payments is called interest cover. Interest cover measures the number of times the interest cost is divided into the net operating profit. Higher ratios are rewarded with lower interest rates.

net assets

Now we have moved on from the trading account and the income statement to the balance sheet. A balance sheet is a statement of an enterprise's financial position at a point in time. It shows the two sides of the financial situation - what the business owns and what it owes. Expressed as an equation, total assets equal the sum of non-interest-bearing debt, shareholders' equity and interest-bearing debt. The net assets element of the balance sheet is calculated by deducting non-interest-bearing debt (current liabilities) from the total assets. This is a useful element to measure because it can be controlled by people who do not necessarily have any influence on formal borrowings and their terms. So, a key measurement is the return on net assets. Return on net assets is measured by dividing net operating profits by net assets. Higher returns indicate greater efficiency, which lead to reduced balance sheet funding requirements, thus leading to reduced interest charges.

Let us examine the components of the return on net assets formula (ROA)

download: net asset management

This Microsoft Excel spreadsheet is designed as an interactive teaching tool. It uses high-level trading data to demonstrate how a target return on net assets can be achieved. It teaches the formulae related to return on sales (ROS), asset turn (AT) and return on net assets (ROA) and their inter-relationship.

The objective is to optimise the return on net assets (ROA). This can be done by addressing one or more combinations of these components:

- increasing net operating profits
- reducing fixed assets
- reducing inventory
- reducing receivables
- increasing payables

By using these formulae, it means that if margins in a business are high, asset turn can afford to be lower to achieve a desired ROA. Conversely, if margins are low, asset turn needs to be higher to achieve the desired ROA. Incentivising employees responsible for optimising ROA is probably a good investment.

funding

The final area to investigate on how to improve the quality of earnings of a business is to focus on how it is funded. There are two key funding ratios:

return on equity
This ratio measures the percentage of taxed profits earned from the shareholders' equity at the beginning of a financial year.

debt / equity
This ratio presents the proportion of interest-bearing debt to shareholders' equity in your business, which collectively equals the net assets. A value less than 1 means that the business has less interest-bearing debt than shareholders' equity in the business. This ratio is driven by policy and is used to determine the strategic sustainable growth rate of your business. This ratio is usually considered when business expansion is on the table and, of course, when determining the value dividend paid to shareholders.

make the financial model a decision checkpoint

Develop your own financial model that allows you to measure the dynamics of your business idea. I have created a Microsoft Excel spreadsheet available for download, which can form the basis of that model. It will also serve as a tool to learn from when applying the lessons from this chapter.

download: dynamics
This Microsoft Excel spreadsheet is designed as an interactive teaching tool. It allows for the evaluation of changes to various business elements such as: contribution, expenses, interest and taxation, working capital and funding, on the profitability of a business. Real learning value is derived when used in

conjunction with other downloadable spreadsheets such as the funding calculator, net asset management and working capital.

download: funding calculator

This Microsoft Excel spreadsheet is designed as an interactive teaching tool. It allows for the evaluation of changes to various balance sheet elements such as: total assets, non-interest-bearing debt and interest-bearing debt. It shows how interest paid is affected by the structure of debt and equity on a business' balance sheet.

download: working capital

This Microsoft Excel spreadsheet is designed as an interactive teaching tool. It uses high-level trading data to teach the formulae related to days inventory, days receivables and days payables. It demonstrates how cash flow is affected by setting realistic targets for each working capital element.

Alternatively, consider purchasing my BizzDynamics app, which also allows you to learn and apply these lessons, but is much easier to use.

BizzDynamics is a business learning simulator. It is designed to show how changes to key business elements, such as contribution, expenses, asset levels and funding strategies impact the financial results of a trading business. You will learn by simulation and you can evaluate the results in the reports tab of the app, where these dynamics are explained.

about BizzDynamics

The app requires that seven specific steps to be completed:

- setup
- employment
- expenses
- fixed assets
- other income
- unit sales model
- funding calculator

Each step has four components:

- base assumptions: requires the input of basic business assumptions
- summary: summarises the step's data, which is included in the financial reports
- base dynamics: allows for changes to those basic assumptions
- forecast dynamics: allows for future adjustment to the base assumptions

This presents a set of financial reports, which includes:

- income statement
- balance sheet
- schedule of expenses
- cash flow
- key ratios.

Each report offers explanations on performance improvement opportunities and these explanations complement BizzBean's learning text feature to assist users in understanding the 'what and why' of each step's input labels as well as a comprehensive list of accounting and business definitions.

financial viability - in summary

Evaluate the financial viability of your business idea, before you decide to start your business. Take time to understand some basic financial terms and very importantly, learn about the importance of cash flow and how it differs from profits.

part 3

plan

You have done your research, and you will have understood the touch-points and assessed the financial viability of your business idea. Now it is time to start planning your business.

business profile

This may be a good time to call for an Innovation Laboratory.

an innovation laboratory

A little story. Many years ago, after doing some alterations to my study at home, I purchased some new furniture with a view to being 'very productive' when I worked from home. The furniture arrived, and I arranged it according to my plans. I packed out all my 'working toys' and began to get the feel of my new home office. A few hours later, my five-year-old son, Gareth, walked in and looked around. Within a few minutes, he challenged the positioning of the furniture. 'Dad, if you have the desk here, you'd have a lot more space'. I was stunned, but he was right. I had taken on the project myself and had given no thought to consulting anybody on my plans, least of all my five-year-old. The lesson I learned was this – bounce ideas off someone and get an opinion. It does not necessarily mean you need to take their advice, but another point of view can only add value. It is your choice to 'use it or lose it'.

Back to business. You are about to start what may be a life-changing adventure. Why not get a bit of help? Call in a few trusted friends and your mentor and brainstorm some ideas. Structure the discussion around the key touch-points, namely your products, customers, suppliers, employees, systems, infrastructure and your values. The outcome is in your hands and may, inter alia, result in you:

- reassessing the execution of ideas
- re-adjusting your long-term plans
- banking ideas for the future

The idea at this stage is to get ideas on how to execute your immediate plans efficiently and not to change your mind.

I learned to make the innovation laboratory a part of my annual business planning cycle. It also proved to be useful whenever I felt the need for 'inspiration'. Not only that, it is a good excuse to get away with the team and work on that much-needed bonding, like fishing!

Once you are ready to develop your business and marketing plans and start the formation of your business, it is a good idea to find some quiet time to develop your two 'Guiding Principles'.

the statement of focus

Write yourself a short paragraph on your business idea. Say exactly what you are going to do and how your products or services are going to solve your customers problems. Be very clear on who your customers are and how you will make money from them. Tell yourself how and when you expect to benefit from your hard work.

At this point it may be a good idea to develop what is called an 'elevator pitch'. An elevator pitch is a short but very powerful statement, which tells a prospective customer exactly what you do and how your products or services will benefit them. The statement must say what exactly what you do and end with a comment 'so that.......' explaining their benefit, precisely. For example:

> BizzBean is a company which develops forecasting,
> budgeting and evaluation software so that entrepreneurs
> can assess a business scenario and make an informed
> financial decision.

Keep these statements in front of you all the time to ensure focus. Often, entrepreneurs start out with an idea but get side-tracked by other forces. Plan the work on your project - allocate specific time to the project if you do not have the resources to do it full-time.

the statement of value

You know what your business is going to do. Now you need to establish the value system which will govern the way you behave towards your stakeholders, especially towards your employees, your customers and your suppliers. The major thrust of these values may change in the future because interpretations are likely to shift over time and because things change. You will need to reassess your values at regular intervals.

The value system within a business is the foundation upon which it will achieve its long-term objectives, and it is imperative that the top-level management of the business wholeheartedly supports and operates within the framework of this value system. The value system must display clarity and focus – 'blue sky' values tend to mislead rather than lead. They must not merely be words on paper – they must become the way the business works.

For example, if quality is a value, it does not help that all effort is placed on the physical quality of the product being manufactured, when the sales quotations are not submitted on time, or are submitted with spelling errors. That quality value must be constantly worked on by the management of the business and it needs to be experienced by all stakeholders.

business profile - in summary

Your reason for starting a business is likely to be your belief that you can solve a customer's problem in your special way. You will employ people who will become very important assets and you will train and guide them to solve customers' problems just the way you would.

Do not lose your focus, especially in the startup phase, and start building your value system early.

business plan

Entrepreneurs require business plans which they will submit to financial institutions to raise finance for their business. In my experience, most startup entrepreneurs have difficulties developing formal business plans for the following reasons:

- they do not know what content to include in their plan
- they are unable to express their ideas fluently
- their plans are generally not understood by the financial institutions
- they are not experienced enough to prepare suitable financial models
- they do not have sufficient funds to employ consultants
- the plan, if prepared by a consultant, lacks sufficient input from the entrepreneur

Financial institutions are generally overwhelmed by the vast number of business plans they receive for review, and consequently many of them go unattended.

I have developed an app solution which addresses these issues in a two-step process. The first step allows entrepreneurs to evaluate the financial viability of their business idea before developing a business plan, and this app is called BizzModel.

BizzModel has some fifty different models covering over four hundred business types, and this number will increase over time.

The second step involves an app called BizzPlan, which is a structured process allowing entrepreneurs to develop their startup business plans with ease. BizzModel seamlessly integrates into BizzPlan, giving entrepreneurs the tools they need to develop a business plan without the need for any professional assistance.

BizzPlan presents a professional business plan in three structured sections:

- executive summary – a five-page document which presents a summary of the business model and its financial forecasts
- touch-points – this section acts as a checklist to ensure that all the costs related to the business touch-points are considered in the financial model
- support schedules – this section lists schedules supporting the various assumptions made in the financial model

Details of six touch-points are described in the checklist section of BizzPlan, while the details of 'owner' (leader) touch-point is included in the executive summary section.

BizzPlan offers two options:

- scripted version - this version allows entrepreneurs to write up a detailed plan of their intended action steps for each sub-element within the various touch-points
- prompted version – this version guides entrepreneurs through sets of multiple-choice statements for each sub-element within the various touch-points and presents a scorecard, making it easier for the financial institutions to evaluate the viability of the business plans

Both versions integrate seamlessly into a chosen BizzModel.

In this chapter, I chose to describe the requirements of the scripted version. The contents are outlined as follows:

section a – executive summary

executive summary

business model

A short paragraph describing the business needs to be written, and your comments should include:
- a description of the business: e.g. manufacturer, importer, distributor or retailer.
- a description of how the products solve customer problems
- a profile of the customers the business will serve

- a description of the market area in which the business competes

business outlook

It requires that you write a short paragraph describing the outlook of the business and your comments should include:

- a comment on why your business will succeed going forward

abridged income statement
- data from BizzModel will automatically update this section

abridged balance sheet
- data from BizzModel will automatically update this section

shareholders' equity
- data from BizzModel will automatically update this section

governance
- use the drop-down menu to select the answers

term-loan structure
- data from BizzModel will automatically update this section

loan-funding conditions
- use the drop-down menu to select the answers

application of funds
- data from BizzModel will automatically update this section

ownership
- complete the section to present ownership details

startup costs
- data from BizzModel will automatically update this section

start date
- data from BizzModel will automatically update this section

legal form of ownership
- use the drop-down menu to select the answers

business objectives
- list short-term objectives

medium-term objectives
- list medium-term objectives

long-term objectives
- list long-term objectives

personal objectives
- use the drop-down menu to select the answers

professional support
- list the names and functions of support team

section b – touch-point checklist

business environment

Write up an explanation under prescribed headings to motivate objectives. Make sure that all considerations are accounted for in the financial model.

research
- consider: source of information; use of professional research units

economics
- consider: currency value; government incentives; tariff protection; tax breaks; specialised skills; segment growth; availability of labour

environmental
- consider: climatic conditions; building codes; legal requirements; licence and bonding; power infrastructure; health and safety; water availability

political
- consider: legislated tariffs and quotas; legislated taxes; specific regulations; unions; benefits from pending

legislation; growth encouragement; benefits from special
bi-lateral trade relationships

management
- use of consultants; use of mentors

products

Write up an explanation under prescribed headings to motivate
objectives. Make sure that all considerations are accounted for
in the financial model.

breakeven – first year
- data from BizzModel will automatically update this section

unit sales forecast
- data from BizzModel will automatically update this section

revenue growth
- data from BizzModel will automatically update this section

product protection
- consider: environmental impact study requirements;
  copyright protection; patent protection; trademark
  protection

product potential
- consider: import replacements; emerging market; changed
  regulations; customer habits; changing technology;
  competitor activity; extended product life cycle

brand management
- consider: brand; market segment; culture; loyalty

features and benefits for customers
- consider: energy; availability; colour attributes; size
  attributes; aftersales service; design features; financial
  backing; price; ease of use; locally manufactured; efficiency;
  productivity; size; quality; international licensing
  agreements; quicker operation; quieter; costs of operation;
  weight

pricing strategy

- consider: currency fluctuations; customer contracts; market forces; volume discounts; recommended retail levels; competitive activity; wholesale margin; royalty component; geographic regions; specific customer trading conditions; accommodate seasonal opportunities

supply chain

- consider: costing system; production bills; outsourced to a sub-contractor; in-line quality management; production methods; production costs; imported content; technology licence; distribution management

inventory management

- consider: finished goods; flammable goods; perishable goods; raw materials; inventory levels determination; inventory levels and seasonal demands

customers

Write up an explanation under prescribed headings to motivate objectives. Make sure that all considerations are accounted for in the financial model.

market share calculator

The market share calculator is designed as a check point to compare the sales forecasted in the BizzModel against your demographic market. The calculator consists of five elements and it is recommended that you understand the requirements of each element before entering any data.

market

This component requires that you enter an estimate of the total market size, its projected growth and the percentage share of each regional market in which you intend to compete. The component only calculates the size of the market in which you intend competing.

primary demographics

Now that you understand the size of the market in which you trade, you need to focus on exactly who your target is in that market. Construct this list by adding your primary demographic targets and estimate the share of each demographic. The component calculates the size of the market in which you intend to compete.

secondary demographics

Now that you have narrowed down your primary market, you need to drill down a bit further to understand any specific secondary demographic, if applicable. Construct this list by adding your secondary demographic targets and estimate the share of each demographic. This component recalculates the size of the market in which you intend to compete, considering the characteristics of your market's secondary demographics.

target market

Now that you have established the estimated size of your target market, you must estimate its usage characteristics. This component assists in calculating the products consumed by your target market. Enter your products estimated annual consumption frequency and the number of items consumed per consumption frequency. Finally, you have a good estimate of how many products are consumed in your target market.

competitor market share

Your target market, however, is shared by competitors so this component requires that you estimate the share of your major competitors. Do this by entering your estimate of their market share, including any change anticipated over the forecast period. The component calculates your market share and compares the size of your share to the sales forecasted in the BizzModel. Take this opportunity to re-evaluate variances presented by this calculator against your forecasts and re-adjust them if necessary.

market distribution
graph data created from competitor share table

download: market share calculator
This Microsoft Excel spreadsheet is designed as an interactive teaching tool. It is designed as a check point to compare forecasted sales against the actual market demographic. The calculator consists of five elements: total market size, primary demographics, secondary demographics, target market and competitors' share. It is designed as a reality check for sales forecasts.

business development strategy
- consider: customer relationship management; website; sales collateral; business via website; business advertising; business via internal sales system; business via direct marketing programmes; business via direct selling activities; business via telemarketing selling; business via independent agents; business via independent representatives; business via owned retail outlets; business via social media programmes; business via tenders

advertising and promotion spend
- use the BizzPlan data forms to complete this information

aftersales support
- consider: structured support; policy; communication

accounts receivable management
- consider: credit granting policy; insured against bad debt; subscribes to a credit assessment service; rules and terms applicable to sales orders; customer selection criteria; employee sales authority

suppliers

Write up an explanation under prescribed headings to motivate objectives. Make sure that all considerations are accounted for in the financial model.

procurement policy

- consider: procurement policy; conditions and use of alternate suppliers; rules and terms applicable to purchase orders; employee purchase authority; product selection criteria; supplier selection criteria

procurement strategy

- consider: tender; reverse auction

accounts payable management

- consider: policy to pay invoices; policy for advanced payments subject to settlement conditions

employees

Write up an explanation under prescribed headings to motivate objectives. Make sure that all considerations are accounted for in the financial model.

employment policy

- consider: a human capital policy; job descriptions; remuneration structure; training and development strategy; discrimination policy; freedom of association; availability of policies

employment strategy

- consider: permanent employment; contract employment; incentives; employee performance measurement

industrial relations strategy

- consider: outsource this function; relationship with all labour unions

employee communications

- consider: business's organization structure; information sharing

remuneration

- consider: performance incentive policy; profit share policy

key management structure
- provide a list of key personnel

personnel deployment
- scheduled in the support schedules

infrastructure

Write up an explanation under prescribed headings to motivate objectives. Make sure that all considerations are accounted for in the financial model.

the premises
- consider: administration facilities; ablution facilities; goods receiving facilities; parking; production facilities; trading facilities; warehousing facilities; workshop facilities; franchisor involvement; communication infrastructure; growth; fire protection; security; ownership status; virtualization

location
- consider: accommodates competitive inertia; accommodates required business trading hours; has convenient customer access - transport route, air, rail, road; has high traffic customer access; is convenient for labour pool

environmental issues
- consider: storage and removal of toxic waste; licences and permits; municipal utilities accounts; pollution control; power requirements; water requirements

financials
- consider: insurance contracts; lease agreements

fixed assets
- fixed assets listed in support schedules

systems

Write up an explanation under prescribed headings to motivate objectives. Make sure that all considerations are accounted for in the financial model.

systems needs' analysis

- consider: need; inter system integration; future business growth; ease of use; speed of implementation; on-going operating costs; on-going support

operations management

- consider: outsource strategy

financial management system

- consider: multiple branch and cost centre sources; market segments; product segments; budgets; future growth; fixed assets

employee management systems

- consider: outsource strategy

customer relationship management system

- consider: competitor activities; customer complaints; remote customer interactions; integration into financial accounting; integration into social media systems; ability to scale

quality system

- consider: beneficial to business performance; ability to scale

computer hardware

- consider: special training requirements; vendor support; off-site redundancy

cloud solutions

- consider: dashboard reporting; inventory management; remote financial transactions

systems cost

- consider: licence costs; initial and ongoing training costs

section c – support schedules

the financial model

The financial forecasts were prepared using an application called BizzModel. This application allowed for the preparation of several scenarios and the most appropriate scenario was selected to support this business plan. The BizzModel application required that relevant forecast data was captured in a structured process as follows:

setup

The setup step required information on the basics of a business including: name, start date, type of business, industry segment, weekdays not worked, other days not worked, vat rate, tax rate and the depreciation rates for fixed assets.

employment

The employment step required information about employees in the business, which information includes: positions and number of people recruited for a position, their cost centre allocation, their start and end dates and their monthly cost to business. The system allowed for parameter adjustments during the forecast period.

expenses

The operating expenses step required information about the type of operating expenses incurred in the business, which includes: description, start and end dates, monthly base cost, its categorisation as either fixed or variable and a percentage to be allocated to cost of sales. The system allowed for parameter adjustments during the forecast period. The startup expenses step required that expenses incurred prior to the commencement of the business.

assets

The fixed assets step required that productive assets were categorised for depreciation rate purposes. These assets were allocated to a cost centre. This step also provided a lease option to finance any productive assets, if required.

other income

This step allows for the capture of several income streams, which may or may not be associated with the primary trading model.

business model

This step initiates the actual trading model specific to this type of business. It processes details of unit sales, unit selling prices, unit cost prices and other associated fixed and variable costs if applicable. The trading model includes a unit price recovery calculation and a breakeven calculation. These calculations are useful in determining a required selling price and a point at which the business breaks even and recovers all fixed costs, excluding financing costs. The system allowed for parameter adjustments during the forecast period. This step initiates the actual trading model specific to this type of business. It processes details of unit sales, unit selling prices, unit cost prices and other associated fixed and variable costs if applicable. The trading model includes a unit price recovery calculator and a breakeven calculator. These calculations are useful in determining a required selling price and a point at which the business breaks even and recovers all fixed costs, excluding financing costs. The system allowed for parameter adjustments during the forecast period.

funding calculator

The funding calculator facilitates the business funding process. It presents the monthly bank balance for the forecast period and presents options on how funding could be obtained. The funding options include the working capital elements such as inventory days, accounts receivable days, accounts payable days and other assets and equity funding in the form of share capital, loan equity and term-loan funding. This step also presents a forecast of earnings and cash resources available to enable a possible dividend calculation. The system allowed for parameter adjustments during the forecast period.

The model produces the reports, which are attached to this business plan.

- income statement
- balance sheet
- schedule of expenses
- cash flow statement
- key ratios

support schedules

This section of the business plan contains schedules and appendices which support elements of the business plan. Some data is imported from the BizzModel, some information requires your input and some information may be appendices to support the business plan.

startup expenses
- data from BizzModel will automatically update this section

schedule of employees
- data from BizzModel will automatically update this section

schedule of fixed assets
- data from BizzModel will automatically update this section

personal financial statement
- use the BizzPlan data forms to complete this information for each partner.

key personnel – resumes
- prepare a concise resume for each partner.

collateral material
Include details and studies used in your business plan; for example:

- brochures and advertising materials
- industry studies
- blueprints and plans
- maps and photos of location
- magazine or other articles
- detailed lists of equipment owned or to be purchased
- copies of leases and contracts
- letters of support from future customers
- any other materials needed to support the assumptions in this plan
- market research studies
- list of assets available as collateral for a loan

download: bizzplan template

This PDF document shows what the BizzPlan business plan template looks like and the type of information it presents. It is a checklist to guide you through the development of your own business plan, if you chose not to use the BizzPlan app.

business plan - in summary

Developing a business plan can be both an expensive and stressful process. Evaluate the financial viability of your business idea before you even think about doing a business plan.

If you do not know how to develop your business plan, use a professional consultant, but insist on being part of the development process and use my guidelines as a template for its development.

part 4

start

Now it is time to act and get that business going. The research has been done, the touch-points of the business are understood and there is confidence in your business plan's financial viability.

call to action

Remember, the business plan consists of words on paper outlining a theoretical call to action. Life, as you know, is not theoretical. Accept that it is unlikely that everything will go according to plan. Accept the need to adapt to unplanned situations and allow for flexibility in executing the plan.

I would like to make some suggestions as to how to deal with that crucial business startup phase. However, while I advocate flexibility, I suggest that the Focus and Value Statements do not change and that the following is adhered to:

- always keep the focus statement in the forefront, ensure focus and do not get side-tracked by other forces
- always live the values - their thrust may change over time, but stakeholders should always be aware of the values which govern the way the business treats them

Starting a business is no doubt one of the most difficult and stressful things you will ever do. Cash resources are strained, systems are untested, employees are insufficiently trained, customers are reticent and suppliers are cautiously keen. This inevitably leads to many long days and lots of stress. Stress may lead to panic, and panic may lead to poor decision-making or a tendency to avoid decisions.

There are key areas of focus under each business touch-point to be discussed but remember that this is a journey. Every step which is tackled along the way becomes a lesson learned, and that includes mistakes. Do not let mistakes be scary. Mistakes are going to happen, so learn from them.

products

Products and services are the lifeblood of any business, and the key objective is to drive sales right from the start. You need to focus on three areas to drive sales during the startup phase. They are:

- attributes
- systems
- salespeople

The reason you start a business is because you have confidence in your products or services. Your research should have justified this confidence, and the obvious thing to do is to highlight how your products' features and benefits solve your customers' problems. It is important for you to focus on those key attributes that differentiate your products from those of your competitors. Develop a metric to highlight how these key attributes stack up against your competitors' products. This tests the original research but also allows important feedback on assumptions.

The startup phase is the time to start the development of distribution systems. Again, it is time to test assumptions. It is time to challenge processes that were thought to be suitable. The objective of these challenges is to improve customer service. It is time to work on process efficiency. This will include processes such as customer contact, credit approval, order processing, distribution, invoicing, debt collection and stock replenishment.

The attributes of products and systems are always enhanced when the business is professionally represented by well-trained representatives. This startup phase offers the opportunity to evaluate what type of customer representation is suitable for the business. Make sure that each representative has the necessary basic selling skills, including tender skills if required. Ensure that they understand the products and their features, and make sure that suitable template proposals are made available. See to it that adequate sales collateral material is effectively distributed and make sure that regular de-briefing/feedback meetings take place. It is my experience that implementing a formal customer relationship management system is an overkill at this stage. Use this time to create sales and to learn about customer requirements. This will make choosing the most appropriate system much easier.

customers

The first focus is to find customers. Besides the fact that they buy the products and services offered by the business, they pay the salaries. Encourage employees to understand that the success of the business lies in their hands because potential customers already have suppliers and a new service or product is simply another choice for them. Customers are only likely to change if a new business can offer a better product at a better price with a better service. Initially, proper systems may not be in place but that must not be used as an excuse to 'miss a deal'. First impressions count with customers, and that includes honesty. If the business cannot execute a customer's request, decline the order. Do not compromise values just to please a customer. Practice a philosophy of 'under promising and over delivering'. Be mindful of the economics of deals, particularly of margins earned. Do not sell to customers who cannot pay. Be tough on credit terms. Cash flow management is always important, but it becomes even more critical in a startup venture.

As stated, proper systems may not be in place. However, this phase should be used to accumulate ideas to be included in future systems to improve customer efficiency. An informal customer relationship management system must therefore be established to collate leads from a website, sales collateral, advertising initiatives, direct selling activities, telemarketing selling, independent agents, representatives, social media programmes and business tenders.

Do not forget aftersales support. Fixing problems quickly and efficiently can win customer support.

My final bit of advice: visit customers frequently and then visit them again and do not stop asking for an order.

suppliers

The relationship suppliers seek to develop with a business is the same as a business seeks to develop with its customers. A good philosophy is to expect suppliers to treat you the same way as you treat your customers. I classify suppliers into three categories as follows:

- cost of sales
- service
- expenses

cost of sales

Cost of sales are those costs which are incurred in the production or acquisition of items or services sold by your business. These suppliers are of a very strategic nature. The business is usually very dependent on them. Building a relationship with them is as important as building relationships with customers. During the startup phase this relationship building exercise is critical because the business would need to exploit opportunities to minimise inventory levels and maximise service levels. That relationship may extend to developing an inventory return program and negotiating favourable startup credit terms. Remember, however, that price and quality must always be in the forefront of negotiations. Make sure this category of supplier understands this right from the start. Consider seeking alternate suppliers just for continuity purposes. The first prize, however, is to build a trusting relationship with one supplier with the objective of optimising the supply chain.

service

Service suppliers include those who ensure that business operations are not affected by lengthy down-time, which may affect production. Building relationships with these suppliers is also very important. These suppliers may be required to perform services at short notice or even after hours. In these cases, while price may be important, the cost of not producing must also be considered. Remember too, quality counts, so do not compromise quality for price. As with suppliers, consider seeking alternate suppliers just for continuity purposes.

expense

Expense suppliers include those who provide items not essential to produce income. Price and convenience should be the criteria when selecting a supplier.

In all cases, however, my advice is to scrutinise every invoice to ensure that charges are aligned to agreed purchase costs. Do not overstock because a supplier may offer a special deal. Watch cash flow and sign all payments, whether paid by bank transfer or cheque. Start the process of optimising the supply chain procurement procedures.

employees

Employees should be recruited for their willingness to share the entrepreneur's values, and now is the time to evaluate their effectiveness. Employment policies have been developed and implemented, and the startup phase is a good time to carry out staff appraisals and determine what measures need to be adopted to improve their skills. It is time to streamline job descriptions and evaluate the effectiveness of remuneration systems. Training requirements will become obvious.

I would like to provide some advice with regards to evaluating the effectiveness of your employees. Hiring mistakes will be made but my advice is to fix these mistakes as soon as possible. Do not put up with poor performers for longer than is necessary. If possible, hire startup employees on short-term performance-based contracts. If family members are included in the employment compliment, treat them no differently to any other employees. Be concerned about employee stress during this phase – overwork is a common phenomenon in startup businesses. Share performance information, good and bad. Making employees feel 'part of the business' goes a long way to improving results.

infrastructure

I recommend starting off modestly. There is a saying 'Image is important, but get the washing done first', which essentially means 'be practical'. We have the convenience of the internet today, which makes virtualisation very possible. To put it in a nutshell, the 'occupational costs' of a business are usually the second highest costs after 'employment costs'. Do not splash out on expensive assets. Think of Apple starting in a garage and Google in a University residence. Unless you have a significant amount of capital and absolute confidence in your service or product, I suggest leasing property on a short-term basis. Make sure that all assets are insured. Loss in the early stage of a business can be devastating.

systems

In my experience, entrepreneurs are not good administrators. Many businesses fail because there was no firm grasp of the numbers. Entrepreneurs go in to business to make money. Therefore, it makes no sense that the business does not keep proper score from the very first day. In the Business Plan checklist, I suggest that an effective accounting system be installed. It does not need to have all the bells and whistles initially, but it must at least invoice goods, control receivables, payables, inventory, expenses and cash flow. It must scale at minimal cost with growth. It is important to have trading information at one's finger tips. I would like to propose that a 'daily operating control' (DOC) be set up. If the system cannot provide the information in a report form, develop a simple spreadsheet to record the following information daily:

- revenue

- gross profit
- cash expenses
- inventory value
- receivables
- payables
- bank balance

It is a good idea to create targets and share this information with employees. It is a great way to motivate for improved performance.

Do not invest in sophisticated systems during the startup phase. Do what is affordable and practical and know the numbers in order to react to situations quickly.

download: doc

This Microsoft Excel spreadsheet is designed as an interactive teaching tool. It is a simple example of a daily operating control sheet (DOC). It compares monthly cumulative results against forecasts for: revenue, gross profit, expenses, net operating profit, inventory, receivables, payables, net assets and the bank balance.

download: cash flow

This Microsoft Excel spreadsheet is designed as an interactive teaching tool. It can be used to forecast daily cash balances in a small trading business. Although simple, it is effective.

leader

live the values

As I said earlier, starting a business is a very challenging time. I can only remind entrepreneurs that the most important thing for you to do is to stay focused on your goals and to live and practice your values. This is the time for leadership. During the startup phase, effective leadership is essential. Life becomes easier when the leader does not panic, communicates well, acts deliberately and sets an example for others to follow.

When I was a young manager, I was profoundly influenced by a programme called 'Towards Excellence', which was developed by Thomas J. Peters and Robert H. Waterman. It was based on their book, 'In Search of Excellence: Lessons from America's Best-Run Companies', in which the programme revolves around five fundamentals. The book is an insightful read, but for this exercise I would like to focus on the fundamental principle of 'instilling unique values', and particularly, 'using mundane tools'. Quoting verbatim from the programme workbook will allow me to share some ideas about developing values within your newly established business. I acknowledge and thank Tom Peters and Robert Waterman for their book, which I have regularly referred to over the past twenty-five years.

So, here they are:

using mundane tools
- allotting time to meet with design engineers regarding progress in new product innovations
- continually telling the truthful story of how, in his or her first year with the company, your boss leads a small skunk-work that produced one of the major products of the company; continually telling and retelling 'stories' of salespeople going to great lengths to satisfy customers
- labelling, for instance, Wednesday a 'no-meeting day' for senior people, to encourage MBWA (managing by wondering around)
- blocking out customer-visit days (or factory-visits days) on your calendar for the next six months
- personally, editing post-meeting minutes to reflect the theme you want to stress
- an executive setting a daily quota for himself on 'thank you' memos or setting weekly quotas on 'theme notes' with, for example, a customer on quality focus
- thinking out visit routines in detail to enhance their thematic impact (e.g. focus on innovation)

- establishing a post-meeting routine of reviewing with the others whether thematic issues stood out in a meeting, regardless of the meeting's official content
- setting aside specific hours of the week for impromptu phone calls to down-the-line employee sources (or customers and vendors) to see how recent messages are being received
- creating a weekly or bi-weekly 'dramatic event' staged to give a public award or otherwise publicise a key value theme

call to action - in summary

This is a very stressful time for you. You are busy creating business opportunities, hiring people, developing systems and attending to many mundane tasks yourself. Do not be afraid to ask for help if you need it. Keep in mind the following advice:

- watch that bank balance
- live within your means
- keep your family close – they should be your support bedrock

keep in touch

My business experience was largely gained before the Internet took over our lives, so I missed out on today's very exciting electronic social media communication streams. In many ways, I am a little grateful, because I had to spend a lot of time talking to management and employees 'face-to-face'. From my observations, face-to-face communication has sadly been replaced by impersonal group communication systems. However, we live in modern times, so we must adapt to modern systems. Whatever methods entrepreneurs choose to use is their choice. What is important, however, is that there is communication. Be careful not to over communicate – people are generally subjected to an overload of information. Do not under communicate either – people want to be kept informed. The secret is to find a balance.

In the startup phase, communication is more operational in nature than strategic. In a later chapter, I will talk about strategy, so for now we will focus on operational communication. Communication is about talking and listening, and about doing this consistently, which means that communication is a two-way street. Messages and instructions come from the top, but information comes from the bottom. Clarity is gained from face-to-face meetings. The purpose of a meeting is to review a situation and react to the situation, which may result in some re-planning.

the 7-minute meeting

I would like to present a meeting process I learned from my NGK Spark Plug principals. It is called the 7-minute meeting, and it is practiced daily within operational structures. I experienced difficulties in implementing it initially, but after some determined perseverance I found success. Some employees lacked confidence in expressing themselves, some cultural issues arose and, of course, there were the inevitable power struggles. Patience is required but the results are worth the efforts. This is how the 7 minutes are utilised:

report back - 2 minutes:
Provide information on previous day's performance, e.g. production, revenue, sales, etc. Provide other relevant information associated to the business, e.g. new appointments, general company information.

answers - 2 minutes:
Provide answers on questions received from the previous day. This gives the leader an opportunity to obtain the correct information. There is no two-way discussion.

questions - 2 minutes:
Receive questions from the team. There is no two-way discussion.

tasks - 1 minute:
This section allows the leader to specify any special assignments or tasks, where performance will be evaluated outside the confines of the meeting.

This process eliminates unnecessary dialogue, which sometimes leads to deviations and off the point discussions. It is efficient and achieves a daily structured two-way communication process.

other meetings

Depending on the leader's style, structured meetings may also be convened to cover departmental and executive (EXCO) communication. I encourage communication, but I would like to suggest that meetings be structured and well controlled. Some suggestions for convening a meeting include:

- prepare an agenda and circulate it well before the meeting is convened
- insist on preparation

- focus on operational issues - performance
- focus on what must be done to change the situation

tips for running a successful meeting

I have learned over my many years in business that the most successful meetings are those that are run by a tough chairperson and that the chairperson does not always need to be the boss. Bosses sometimes like to hear themselves talk. I outline some tips on how to run a successful meeting so that the focus is on:

- saving time and money
- making better decisions
- ensuring commitment to action

Try to practice the following:

meet with the right people
How many times have you attended meetings where the wrong people were present, and the right people were missing? Scrutinise the people who attend your meetings. Be clear on what you expect from each one; then make it clear to them. You might have smaller meetings, but you will get much more done.

start on time
People learn very quickly whether your meetings start on time, or if they do not. Announce that in future your meetings will start exactly on time, and make sure they do. If there are latecomers do not back track. Instead, ask them to respect the starting time. If that does not work, tell everyone that you will start the next meeting on time and when you do, you will lock the door. Most people only need to be locked out once to learn the lesson.

set ground rules
Different types of meeting need to function differently to meet their objectives. You do not run a brainstorming session in the same way you gather data on the causes of a problem. Make the

purpose of the discussion clear and then set ground rules that will help achieve that purpose. For example, if you are gathering data, a useful ground rule is that everyone with input will be heard before actions are put forward. If you make ground rules explicit, people know how they should behave.

appoint a gatekeeper

A gatekeeper makes sure that time is allocated to the important issues, not merely the most topical or personally relevant to someone with a loud voice. The gatekeeper has three responsibilities: agree the agenda with the chairperson of the meeting, agree priorities and agree time allocation for each topic. During the meeting, signal the chairperson on how time is progressing. The gatekeeper can be anyone with some personal discipline and a timepiece. Meetings with effective gatekeeping ensures that appropriate time is allocated to important topics, and it frees up the chairperson to manage the content of the discussion.

write it down

During a meeting make notes or appoint a note taker. Usually all you need are brief notes on the key points of discussion, actions agreed and the people responsible. At a follow-on meeting, start with the action list to ensure continuity and accountability.

stick to the point

Meetings that lose focus are time consuming, frustrating and seldom achieve their purpose. Use paraphrasing behaviour to keep people on track. There are four steps. First, listen carefully so you understand what is being said. Secondly, interject: for example, 'Let me check we've all understood'. Thirdly, paraphrase the essence of what was said. Once you have regained control of the conversation, you can redirect it as necessary. If you use this one behaviour to maintain focus in a meeting, you can achieve twice as much in half the time.

hear from everyone

If you have the right people at the meeting; make sure you hear what they all have to say. Avoid having a few people dominate the discussion by using names and gestures to invite specific people to speak. Be equally specific in asking others to stay quiet and listen to the contributions.

keep it clear

Summarise as you go along. It keeps the conversation on track and ensures that everyone is clear about what has been said. As the meeting progresses, summarising helps you getting to a 'yes', which leads to understanding and commitment that you can consolidate at the end of the discussion.

look backwards and forwards

There is a great difference between collecting information about an issue and deciding what to do about the same issue going forward. For data collection use questions that seek information. To find solutions, use questions that ask for ideas for action. Meetings often get stuck in the asking for and giving of information, without getting to action. It is more comfortable, everyone has their say, but it does not achieve much.

build quality solutions

Do not let meetings degenerate into a win-lose fight. This happens when several ideas are put on the table and participants defend their own stance until someone wins. The winner who has the loudest voice takes all, even though the idea may not be the best. The losers are unlikely to have any commitment to the idea, which impacts negatively on the implementation, at which point the whole process starts over. Encourage people to listen to and build on each other's ideas, resulting in commitment to better quality solutions.

Finally, get rid of those cell phones during meeting time – introduce a cell phone break.

keep in touch - in summary

Learn to communicate and learn to share information – you will be better off for it in the long-term.

measure

In a previous chapter, I talked about the importance of having information at hand in the form of a DOC. In the next chapter, Keep Score, I will be talking about the importance of maintaining proper accounting records. I would now like to focus on how to use information to improve profitability. In another previous chapter, Financial Viability, we discussed how profits can be improved by:

- optimising the trading mix
- reducing expenses
- reducing interest and tax rates
- optimising working capital efficiency and
- optimising funding efficiency

The touch-points within a business can now be explored to see how we can interrogate data and look for opportunities to improve profit efficiency. For this exercise, I would like to combine products and customers into a single discussion focus, and the reason will become obvious.

products and customers

When I assist entrepreneurs to evaluate the efficiency of their business, my first task is to extract specific data from their sales journal into a pre-prepared Microsoft Excel spreadsheet and use Excel's power, particularly its PivotTable, to analyse the data. Most times, I get a 'wow' from clients, because they have never thought of 'stepping outside' and looking at their business objectively and without emotion. Let us explore a few examples of things to look for:

- are margin contributions from the largest customers below average?
- are credit terms to these customers extended beyond normal terms?

- are distribution costs to customers measured?
- are margin contributions from highest volume or highest value items below average?

There may very well be good reasons, but very often, in my experience, it is the customer calling the shots on price and not the business promoting their service value.

I present a schedule of information, which when extracted into a spreadsheet, can be manipulated for information purposes. This information must be extracted from a sales transaction file for a specific evaluation period. Each transaction will include the following data:

- date - the date of the transaction
- item code - the code of the item being sold
- item description - the description of the item
- items sold - the number of items sold
- item price – the realised price for the item sold
- item cost – the unit cost of the item sold
- item inventory – the aggregate value of the item's inventory value at a point in time
- customer code – the code of the customer to whom the item is sold
- customer name – the customer's name to whom the item is sold
- customer receivable - the aggregate value of the customer's indebtedness at a point in time

This information can be manipulated to obtain the following information:

- customer – revenue and gross profit contribution, gross profit margin contribution and receivables efficiency
- item – revenue and gross profit contribution, gross profit margin contribution and stock turn efficiency

An exercise like this, done regularly, allows you to 'clear the cupboard' of unprofitable products and customers. Do not just 'clear' without evaluating the consequences. This may be an opportunity to re-negotiate business terms with some customers.

This Microsoft Excel spreadsheet is designed as an interactive teaching tool. It is an example on how product contribution can be analysed for each customer. It can be adapted to accommodate many additional records, which ideally can be imported from an accounting system.

suppliers

In an earlier chapter I suggested that suppliers be categorised into three categories, namely, cost of sales, service and expenses suppliers.

Similar to the way in which sales information is extracted from a sales journal, product purchases should also be analysed using an evaluation tool, such as a Microsoft Excel PivotTable. Each purchase transaction will include the following data:

- date – order date
- date – receipt date
- item code - the code of the item being purchased
- item description - the description of the item
- items purchased - the number of items purchased
- item cost – the unit cost of the item purchased
- item inventory – the aggregate value of the item's inventory value at a point in time
- item category – the category allocated to the item
- suppliers' payable - the aggregate value of the indebtedness to the suppliers at a point in time

This information can be used to create an index for each supplier, which can be used to evaluate their efficiency. A scorecard can be developed, which could be weighted to emphasise the importance of a specific element within a supplier category. Suggested elements of the scorecard would include:

- price – rate the unit price compared to other suppliers
- price change cycle – rate the frequency of price changes
- transparency – rate the suppliers' willingness to provide justification for price changes
- days to complete order – rate the frequency on which suppliers' hit order due dates, including early supply
- quality – rate the product quality against others
- returns – rate the suppliers' willingness to accept damaged goods, including transport costs
- credit terms – rate the suppliers' willingness to grant favourable credit terms

An exercise like this will require some intervention to systems. It becomes worth it, however, when suppliers are presented with a factual performance scorecard. This creates an opportunity to re-negotiate business terms with some suppliers.

employees

I would like to share a few quotes from Sir Richard Branson.

'Train people well enough so they can leave, treat them well enough so they don't want to.'

'The way you treat your employees is the way they will treat your customers.'

'Clients do not come first. Employees come first. If you take care of your employees, they will take care of the clients.'

While I agree with Sir Richard, I firmly believe that the performance of all employees should be measured on a regular basis. I am not a fan of job descriptions. I prefer to use a results-based program, where actual results are measured against agreed outputs. Results must be measured consistently and regularly. This allows for some training intervention if necessary. In this way, good people will be rewarded and poor performers should be eliminated. Get rid of poor performers at an early stage – the first loss is the best loss.

Let us investigate some areas where performance can be measured.

productivity

Productivity is a measure of output per unit of input. Employee productivity can be measured in several ways. For example, a motor dealership will measure the number of vehicles sold, the revenue and the gross profit derived per salesperson employed for specific periods. These measurements will be compared to previous periods and even to industry benchmarks. The obvious objective is to ensure that productivity levels are continuously improved over time. These objectives are achieved by improving systems within the business and by the development of employees.

Determine benchmark productivity standards within your business. Do this in conjunction with employees and consider incentivising improvements.

efficiency

Cost efficiency is a measure of input cost against a measure of output value. For example, that same motor dealership will measure the cost of salespeople against the total value of revenue and gross profit earned by them. The lower the ratio means the business is more efficiently run. These ratios always present management with decision challenges, which may result from issues of low productivity. Management now has the data to make decisions for corrective action.

assessments

Identify averages and ratios of interest to measure performance of salesperson(s) (using the performance variables above). These may include aggregated salesforce, individual salesperson or product line figures that can be used to assess performance of sales territories, individual products or product lines, or salespeople. Order-call ratio per salesperson (number of orders per salesperson number of calls made per salesperson x 100); average sales per salesperson (total salesperson sales in dollars; number of sales of salesperson); average number of sales per client size; number of sales for client size ratio (number sales to client; client size index)

Identify averages and ratios of interest to measure cost of salesperson(s) or total territory costs or product line costs (using the performance variables above); salesperson costs-sales ratio (salesperson cost; sales in dollars generated by sales person x 100); territory costs-sales ratio (territory / store costs; sales in dollars generated by territory / store x 100).

infrastructure

Infrastructure is the term used to encompass the assets within your business from which you derive income. It includes buildings, vehicles, plant and equipment, furniture and fittings, computer equipment and so on. These assets may be owned or leased.

It is difficult to understand why many companies spend a lot of money buying or leasing these assets and do not care for them. The lack of routine maintenance can cause down-the-line production stoppages, which may well be costlier in terms of lost revenue than the cost of maintenance. Caring for these assets will go a long way to extend their lifespan and improve productivity. It will also add equity value to the business. This additional equity must also be measured. Systems, however, must be in place to measure the efficiency of these assets, either at their original cost value or their replacement value. For example; the operating costs, including maintenance of an item of plant, may be greater than the cost of the finance and operating costs of a new replacement item; the property you trade from may not yield the turnover per square or cubic metre you could achieve from a perceivably more expensive property. Very often, perceived cost is the benchmark for acquiring an asset.

systems

How does one measure systems? Systems are put in place to measure the performance of the other touch-points. I believe, however, that a key measurement of the success of a business is how well it runs when the startup leaders are not around.

There's a saying 'work on your business, not in your business'.

One of the key objectives of a leader should be to build the business so that it can function efficiently without being dependant on the leader. In this way, the leader is building up that asset of value. In an earlier chapter, I outlined my achievements at NGK Spark Plugs. When I took over the management of the company, it was not in good shape. Besides the fact that the NGK brand was struggling, the company did not have a good reputation for supplying products to its customers. I was new to the motor components industry and my lack of experience showed when I fired the entire quality department because I thought it was an unnecessary overhead. My action drew the attention of an important customer in The Ford Motor Company, and within days I was faced with a factory deputation to whom I had to justify my action. I remember that meeting very well. Ford insisted that I reinstate a quality department or lose their business, and I refused because I could not see what value it added to the business. One might say it was a standoff.

A few days later, I was invited to lunch by senior executives of Ford. The Ford executives had obviously listened to my reasoning and understood my reluctance to invest in what I termed 'a deep hole'. After lunch, I toured their factory and I was given an oversight of their operating processes. My eyes were opened and so was my mind. To this day, I think that the Ford executives had a hidden agenda. They needed NGK and they believed they could work with me to achieve a common objective.

I had a major change in mind-set. I suddenly realised that quality was not only in the attributes of the product, it was a lot more than that. Ford made me realise that quality was 'holistic'. In order to become holistic, I did not need a quality department, I needed a quality company. With Ford's support, I re-built all the systems within the company. Every process was defined and documented. Each employee was trained to operate within the defined processes. The result: in a space of two years, the company was awarded Ford's highest quality recognition. The company only had one person in the quality department, but the rest of the employees were all 'quality managers'.

To summarise what I learnt:

- document each process: what is done, how is it done and why is it done
- review: ensure systems are relevant – look to improve efficiencies
- train: ensure employees are well trained and motivated to seek efficiency
- keep things simple: there is no need to over-engineer systems
- integrate: strive to have fewer systems – discourage the use of spreadsheets, unless for analysis purposes
- dashboards: build systems to present real-time information – sort out problems quickly

It is essential to create systems that make the business work efficiently, but also to ensure that the relevant information is always available to measure performance, be it positive or negative.

leader

Startup entrepreneurs have only two measurement criteria:

- financial performance of the business
- personal objectives set when starting the business

The performance of the business will be measured from the presentation of regular financial results. The personal objectives are usually a private matter, and these can only be measured and acted upon by the leader at the appropriate time.

measure - in summary

Numbers do not lie!

Everything you do in your business should have a measurable outcome. Develop measurement systems over time and use the numbers to maximise value and minimise waste. Use the numbers to make smart decisions.

keep score

When I play a game of golf with my friends, I keep a track of my score for three reasons. Firstly, I want evidence of my score in order to claim my 'winnings'. Secondly, I want to evaluate my personal comparative performance, and thirdly, I want to analyse exactly what I did where, so I can work on the specific details of my game to improve future performances.

In some ways, running a business is no different to playing a game of golf or playing a football match. Scores are tallied up instantly and when the game is over, the winner and loser are declared. That is not usually the end of the game, because a detailed analysis is now required. Each play and each player, as well as the coach's strategy, is critically scrutinised, all of which are backed up with detailed statistics.

Why?

It is simple. The objective is to make improvements, and that is done by learning from past actions.

I am blessed to have had a career where I experienced an explosive transformation in the speed of processing data into information. Hand-written invoices, prepared by a shopkeeper, have been replaced by real-time invoices generated by customers. The consolidation of financial statements for a large public company has been reduced from two months to a matter of minutes, in spite of an explosion in the increase in transaction volumes.

There are two important reasons to set up good financial systems within a business:

- immediate information: this allows the management to evaluate situations quickly and make appropriate decisions accordingly

- governance: this maintains an accurate record of the assets and liabilities of your business

The financial systems should have the ability to present an accurate running score of key elements of the business, where the opponent is the budget or a forecast. It should also provide details for analysis and review. Ideally, there are certain things which need to be in place to keep score within a business.

The financial system in use should consider the key attributes which I suggested in an earlier chapter. At any one time, the system needs to cater for all the appropriate financial needs of the business, e.g. sales, debtors' management, purchases, supplier and inventory management, general ledger and reporting. It will be an integrated system which allows data to be captured only once, resulting in all the appropriate accounting transactions being automatically updated. It will be easy to use and will present appropriate reports on demand.

Implementing a successful financial system needs to consider the following:

scorekeeper

There is no point in having a fantastic financial system unless it is not well administered. I am very critical of entrepreneurs who do not value the importance of maintaining an efficient accounting and administration system. A wise entrepreneur will partner with a dynamic financial professional, a scorekeeper, who will see to it that the books always present an accurate up-to-date financial position of your business. In business, a scorekeeper is the chief financial officer (CFO). The CFO must get into the habit of doing 'today's things today' and striving to get things 'right first time'. Apart from ensuring that the books are always kept up date, the CFO must make sure that issues such as taxation and statutory returns are duly submitted. The CFO must be acquainted with all up-to-date legislation which is relevant to your business and the industries it serves. The CFO must also attend to all secretarial and audit issues. Furthermore, the CFO should build and maintain strong relationships with funding institutions and keep them informed, either formally or informally, on the performance of your business.

information maintenance

In the previous chapter, I talked about the importance of implementing and maintaining systems within an enterprise. Poor maintenance of systems could result in unnecessary losses. For example, a supplier could advise a change in price on a component. If that price change is not registered in the costing system, e.g. a bill of material, as soon as it is received, the production costs would be incorrectly calculated and an opportunity to renegotiate a selling price change with customers may be delayed or missed. These situations could have the consequence of eroding margins. I believe it is therefore important to maintain information in the systems to protect margins. Let us explore some areas where information maintenance should become systematic:

product costs
Maintenance of product costs will include all traded products and may also involve the update of supplier contracts, both of which could involve the update of bills of materials.

selling prices
Maintenance of selling prices will also involve the update of various customer or product price metrics and, of course, supply contracts.

creditors
Maintenance of creditors will include an audit of suppliers listed as creditors on the database from time to time. You will need to verify their contact details as listed. Question the necessity of their listing, especially if they have not been a regular supplier. Check their bank account details – very often fraudsters make use of fictitious creditors and change bank account details (on

the bank payment system) to divert funds to their personal accounts. Updates and verification of relevant personnel contact details should be done on a regular basis.

debtors

It is also a good idea to audit customers listed as debtors on the database from time to time. Verify their contact details as listed. Question the necessity of their listing, especially if they have not been a regular customer. Update and verify relevant personnel contact details. Review their credit status.

contracts register

Even when your business is small, it is a good idea to set up a contracts' register, where review and renewal dates are scheduled. Make sure that this register is inspected regularly, or if the system is in an electronic format, that it sends out reminders to appropriate administrators. This register may include various leases signed for either property or other movable assets, if they are not separately recorded.

fixed assets register

The accounting system will usually include a fixed assets' register. If not, some form of manual system (Excel spreadsheet) needs to be maintained. In either system, the register needs to maintain the minimum critical details of each fixed asset, such as description, supplier, purchase date, purchase cost and depreciation rate. These values will be included in the monthly financial statements.

download: assets

This Microsoft Excel spreadsheet is designed as an interactive teaching tool. It has two components: a simple asset register and a lease asset register. It can work for a small business, but it will need to have rows inserted to accommodate additional asset items. This is easily done.

The fixed assets component aggregates the monthly depreciation and the balance sheet value of each fixed asset item, while the leased asset component aggregates the monthly lease values of each leased item.

payroll system

The administration of the payroll may be outsourced or administered by a specific department within your business. Either way, it is important to verify that the employees being paid are employed by your business and that their pay rate is that which was agreed to in the employment contract. A regular check should be made to ensure that the employment cost is allocated to the correct cost centre.

budgeting and forecasting

I will discuss the annual budgeting process in a future chapter. Let us assume, however, that your business has its annual budget in place. It would be the CFO's responsibility to ensure that all relevant department managers are aware of their targets and that these targets are broken down into monthly values. It would be the CFO's responsibility to track and react to variances because collectively they impact your business's cash flow requirements.

daily operational control (doc)

In a previous chapter, I talked about the importance of having trading information at one's finger tips and I proposed the establishment of a 'daily operating control' system (DOC). It would be the CFO's responsibility to present this information to all department managers daily. The DOC is the monthly budget divided by the number of trading days for each month. The objective of this report would be to present the relevant department managers with their trading position at any point in a month. It would present a variance 'to date' and calculate what the daily values are required to achieve the monthly budget value.

Ideally, the DOC would be presented in some form of 'dashboard' system and would be made available to key executives via an Intranet or the Internet. It would be presented in such a way that departmental information would be available to each relevant manager and the results would be dynamically consolidated to present the entire enterprise's financial information. This report will allow management to evaluate the trading results of your business compared to the plan on a continuous basis and its impact on critical planning issues, which obviously involves cash flow.

download: doc

This Microsoft Excel spreadsheet is designed as an interactive teaching tool. It is a simple example of a daily operating control sheet (DOC). It compares monthly cumulative results against forecasts for: revenue, gross profit, expenses, net operating profit, inventory, receivables, payables, net assets and the bank balance.

management accounts

The preparation of the monthly management accounts is usually a big highlight for most enthusiastic financial departments. I expect three things from a CFO when preparing the monthly financial accounts:

accuracy

Ensure that the accounts are accurate. This means that the various departmental managers need to sign off on the accuracy of their results. Mistakes happen during the data processing phase and having an extra 'eye' helps to sort out issues. Encourage 'down-the-line' employees to challenge the numbers. This can be a very 'challenging' experience but two things happen: firstly, the accounts will be accurate, and secondly, people learn, which brings me to my second point.

education

This is a good time to explain the meaning of 'the numbers'. In an earlier chapter I talked about how focusing on five key areas would contribute to improving the financial performance of an enterprise. The CFO should use the appropriate key area lesson to teach the 'down-the-line' employees how their actions could improve results. Patience will be required. Remember, they are not necessarily accountants. Sharing and teaching does wonders to performance improvement, especially if there are some incentives on the table.

analysis

Again, it is time to explain the numbers to the executive committee and the board. The CFO must produce a succinct report, which highlights the salient features of the results. This report must detail variances against budget and present a summary of risks and opportunities. This report will be summarised from various data banks, which data can be further 'drilled down' for finer analysis – something I call 'circumcising mosquitoes'. The report is strengthened by the fact that it has direct input from the various line managers. Adding appropriate charts would add value to the report.

I have shared an example on how I prefer my financial accounts to be presented. The key to my presentation preference is that the account's monthly results and the year-to-date results are compared to the budget values. I also like to ensure that each month's trading results are presented side by side, which facilitates easy monthly comparisons.

The management accounts 'pack' should consist of the following:

- balance sheet
- income statement
- cash flow statement
- trading account - departmentalised
- manufacturing account – if applicable

- schedule of expenses - departmentalised
- key ratios

download: management accounts

This PDF document illustrates a suggested presentation of monthly management accounts. Most modern accounting systems have very powerful report writing features, which allow for flexible reports designs.

This presentation demonstrates how monthly values can be compared, progressively, and how each month and the year-to-date results can be compared to a budget forecasts.

audit and verification

The CFO's duty is to ensure that the assets and liabilities of your business are accounted for and valued fairly. To achieve this, the CFO must ensure that the value of the assets and liabilities recorded in the general ledger agree to the various sub-ledgers, and that those sub-ledger values are accurately recorded and verified.

To achieve this, the CFO must put in place a monthly process whereby all the assets and liabilities of your business are verified. This will include:

inventory

A physical count of inventory, goods in transit and work-in-progress should be done monthly. If a monthly inventory count is not feasible, the introduction of a structured cycle stock count system should be considered, ensuring that fast moving and high-value items are counted frequently. A full 'wall-to-wall' stock count should be done at least twice a year. The physical count results must be compared to theoretical stock list, which must be adjusted accordingly. The adjusted variances must be recorded as an inventory adjustment and accounted for in the income statement.

download: inventory analysis

This Microsoft Excel spreadsheet is designed as an interactive teaching tool. It analyses the effect of aging inventory in a business. It allows simulation of days inventory to calculate the effect on cash flow and interest costs.

debtors

Each debtor's account should be 'reconciled' on a monthly basis to ensure that customer payments are correctly allocated to their ledger account. Reasons should be speedily sought for any unpaid invoices.

download: receivables analysis

This Microsoft Excel spreadsheet is designed as an interactive teaching tool. It analyses the effect of aging receivables in a business. It allows simulation of days receivables to calculate the effect on cash flow and interest costs.

creditors

Each creditor's account should be 'reconciled' to the suppliers' debtors statement monthly to ensure that all goods received for purchase orders are correctly allocated to their ledger account, and that all payments made to the supplier are recorded on their debtor's statement.

fixed assets

Each fixed asset must be reconciled to the fixed assets register annually.

bank

The bank balance recorded in the general ledger must be reconciled with the bank's statement balance monthly.

payroll liabilities

Payroll liabilities such as pension deductions, employee taxes and general deductions must be reconciled to the various general ledger accounts.

other assets and liabilities

Other assets and liabilities may include loans to third parties and loans from financial institutions, which must be verified on a regular basis or at least twice a year.

Carrying out the above and implementing structured internal controls, including segregating the duties of employee members involved in payments, debtors and creditors, will put the CFO in a good standing with the auditors and shareholders of your business. It may even result in some reduction in audit fees.

at a moment's notice

Because the books are always accurate and up-to-date, your business will be able to apply for funds when business expansion is on the table, without doing much 'extra' work. An accurate and up-to-date set of books will also impress an investor, should you decide to sell all or part of your business.

information technology

The CFO must ensure that all information within your business is secure and easily retrievable. Duties in this respect would include maintaining software licensing, maintaining computer hardware and ensuring that all computer data is backed up and stored, either in the cloud or at a redundant off-site data centre.

keep score - in summary

This small bit of advice about 'keeping score' should convince entrepreneurs that keeping an accurate scoreboard of all key elements of their enterprise and critically reviewing performance regularly, is in their best interest.

part 5

touch-points

Your business has reached a point of stability. You have put in a lot of hard work and you have made a few mistakes. Your systems and processes are in place and now it is time for you to focus on adding value to those touch-points.

products

Put yourself in your customers' shoes and ask yourself the following questions:

- what do they want from my products?
- how do my products meet their needs?
- where do they find my products?
- how do I differentiate my products services from those of my competitors?
- what perceived value should they expect from my products?

Ask yourself one final question:

- how do my products solve my customers' problems?

Now, let us explore how you can start thinking about adding more value to your customers. In a previous chapter, I discussed the importance of maintaining and evaluating data. Let me now introduce you to a very practical reason for doing this by introducing you to the BCG model.

BCG model

This model was developed by the Boston Consulting Group. It is based on the product life cycle theory and is used to determine what priorities should be given in the product portfolio of a business unit. It assumes that a business would, in the long-term, create value by building up a portfolio of products that contain both high-growth products in need of cash inputs and low-growth products that generate a lot of cash. The model has two dimensions: market share and market growth. The basic idea behind it is that the bigger the market share a product has, or the faster the product's market grows, the better it is for the company. The model helps to understand that a one-size-fits-all-approach to strategy cannot be adopted for each product.

Let us examine the components of the model.

stars – high market share in a high growth market

Stars operate in high growth industries and maintain a high market share. Stars are both cash generators and cash users. They are the primary units in which the company should invest its money, because stars are expected to become Cash Cows and generate positive cash flows. Not all Stars generate cash flows, however. This is especially true in rapidly changing industries, where new innovative products can soon be ousted by new technological advancements, so a Star, instead of becoming a Cash Cow, becomes a Dog.

cash cows – high market share in a low growth market

Cash Cows are the most profitable brands and should be 'milked' to provide as much cash as possible. The cash gained from Cows should be invested into Stars to support their further growth. According to the growth-share matrix, corporates should not invest in Cash Cows to induce growth. They should only support them so that they can maintain their current market share. Again, this is not always the truth. Cash Cows usually reside in large corporations or strategic business units that are capable of innovating new products or processes, which may become new Stars. If there was no support for Cash Cows, they would not be capable of such innovations.

dogs – low market share in a low growth market

Dogs hold low market share compared to competitors and operate in a slowly growing market. In general, they are not worth investing in because they generate low or negative cash returns. But this is not always the truth. Some Dogs may be profitable for a long period of time, or they may provide synergies for other brands or strategic business units. They may simply act as a defence to counter competitor moves. Therefore, it is always important to perform a deeper analysis of each brand or strategic business unit to make sure that they are not worth investing in or they must be divested.

question marks – low market share in a high growth market
Question Marks are the brands that require much closer consideration. They hold low market share in fast growing markets, consuming large amounts of cash and incurring losses. They have the potential to gain market share and become a Star, which would later become a Cash Cow. Question Marks do not always succeed, and even after a large amount of investment, they struggle to gain market share and eventually become Dogs. Therefore, they require very close consideration to decide if they are worth investing in or not.

The BCG Model's strategy is summarised as follows:

stars
- stars are leaders in the business, so they should generate large amounts of cash
- stars are in balance with net cash flow - attempt to hold share, because the rewards will be a cash cow if market share is maintained

cash cows
- cash cows should have high profits and cash generation because of the low growth
- investments in cash cows should be low while profits are high
- cash cows are the foundation of a business

dogs
- avoid and minimize the number of dogs in the business
- be aware of expensive 'turn around plans' for dogs
- liquidate dogs if they do not deliver cash

question marks
- question marks demand cash to maintain or grow market share, and have the worst cash flow characteristics
- if nothing is done to change the market share situation, question marks simply absorb cash, and as growth stops, they become dogs

- either invest heavily in question marks to increase market share; or sell them off; or invest nothing and generate whatever cash it can - in other words, increase market share or deliver cash

Download the BCG Map.

download: bcg.pdf
This is a PDF graphic illustration, which explains the theory of the BCG Model.

Now let us go back to adding value.

Use the BCG Map to plot the relative positions of your products and those of your competitors. This will enable you to develop strategies for each product, whose objectives are to ensure relevance, growth and profitability. There is no magic blueprint to determine what strategy should be adopted to achieve these objectives. However, you can do no harm by studying the strategies deployed in both the motor and mobile phone industries.

Both industries are fiercely competitive. They strive for brand relevance, position their products to capture a specific market and balance their efforts to make profits. Both industries, in order to remain successful, do the following three important things:

- measure and evaluate the market positions of each of their products in minute detail
- listen to their customers to understand product relevance
- consistently innovate by introducing features to differentiate their products from those of their competitors

What do these companies do then to get us to buy their products?

They use four weapons, crafted in component combinations, to lure us to become customers. These weapons are:

features

The first thing they do, is to choose the exact market in which they can claim relevance. In the motor industry, for example, some manufacturers choose not to compete in the commercial segment of the industry, while some will be in that segment but will choose only to compete in a sub-section of the segment. They do this for a variety of reasons - for example, they may only have the skills or funds to compete in a specific sub-section. That market determines their products and, of course, who their customers are.

So, what would a manufacturer do to remain relevant, grow or protect market share and protect profits?

They would focus on their features.

They would make sure that their products are equipped with features relevant to their various target markets. A mobile phone manufacturer, for example, will exclude a high-end feature such as high-speed internet connectivity and a camera from a device, which is aimed at a 'phone only' customer, while it will use its 'unique' features to promote its expensive high-end devices. At the same time, however, it will continue to enhance its usability features, in all devices, to promote its brand.

Features may also include those which may be classified as the 'soft' type. These important features may include things like add-ons, packaging (design and sizing) and warranties, upgrades and exchange plans, to name a few.

Evaluate the introduction of new products but do not assume that your customers are necessarily your target market.

In your business, your products should be consistently reviewed for their competitive relevance. Your products should always evolve to solve your customers' problems. Do not assume that you know what your customers' problems are. Ask them and keep asking them if your products are relevant. They would like you to produce a variant of your products as their 'house brand' – this may be a profitable opportunity. Do not make changes for the sake of making changes. There is a very famous case study about how Coca-Cola changed their recipe without consulting their customers. Read about it in a book entitled 'The Other Guy Blinked: How Pepsi Won the Cola Wars' by Jesse Kornbluth and Roger Enrico, published in October 1986. Do not assume that your existing customers are necessarily a good target when you are considering the introduction of new products. Your customers do not owe you exclusive loyalty.

price

Price can be used as a very powerful weapon to increase both profitability and market share. In the Financial Viability chapter, I referred to the fact that earning a higher margin on a product made overhead recovery much easier. Of course, that is true when you rely on a single product. Once you expand your product range, you have an opportunity to use your product mix to increase your market share, and even with slightly lower margins on some products, the aggregate contribution may improve financial results. It could be a risky strategy.

Use this weapon to add value to your customers. Develop customer-specific price lists to increase market share and net aggregate contributions. Do your homework on estimating each customer's contribution from their product mix and make sure that you are consistently analysing your aggregate net contribution.

promotion

The management of brands and products these days is becoming a very dynamic science. The various social media platforms allow a marketing executive to target customers and potential customers with precise accuracy. To be successful, however, the marketing executive needs to be armed with dynamic information in the form of sales statistics, customer demographics, pricing, contributions and relevance surveys. The marketing executive should become the custodian of the business' BCG map and assume the responsibility for adding value to the business by:

- analysing the demographics of historical sales to explore opportunity gaps
- utilising modern marketing platforms to increase the efficiency of the marketing spend
- introduce customer loyalty systems
- introduce the concept of brand and product management to improve product market share and product contribution

The strategic direction of the business needs the contribution of the marketing executive.

getting it to the market

We are living in a very disruptive world. The notion that a business needs to have its own administrative centre, warehouse and salesforce, for example, is being challenged by so many new disruptive technologies, which are designed to reduce costs and improve efficiency. In a future chapter on Systems, I talk about the possibility of optimising a supply chain to improve efficiency, reduce costs and improve customer loyalty. Let us now focus on what you can do about adding value to where and how your customers can get your products and services.

There was a time when we 'had' to go the fast food outlet, in person, to get that pizza – today, there is a new industry that specialises in getting that pizza to your home or office. There was a time when we went to the book store to buy that new bestseller – today, we can download that book onto any one of many reading devices in seconds. There are many, many more examples, where the use of the Internet has disintermediated the buyer from the seller.

You have a challenge - you need to balance competitiveness against disintermediating your customers. There is no general or magic formula to improve your competitiveness. You need to implement solutions that improve efficiencies without upsetting your customers. You need to be innovative and you need to consult your customers before you introduce any radical or disruptive distribution systems.

products - in summary

Real value in your business is realised when you:

- efficiently exploit the potential contribution of all your products
- continuously solve customer problems through product innovation
- use your product pricing mix to grow your market share with improved margins
- use disruptive technology to improve the efficiency of your supply chain but be sensitive to disintermediating customers

customers

I always told my employees that it was the customers that paid their salaries, not the business. In fact, I went one step further – I demanded that they use a capital 'C' when writing the word customer or client in any business communication. I was obsessed with customer relationships and that obsession was successfully transferred to all my employees, whether they worked in the 'front-line' or if they were involved on a production line. I reminded them that their lives were affected, in some way, by what our customers thought of 'us' collectively.

Now that your business is successful, the most important questions you need to ask yourself about your customers are:

- what are you doing to keep your existing customers?
- what are you doing to get back customers you may have lost?
- what are you doing to get new customers?

In my chapter Call to Action, I referred to a programme called 'Towards Excellence', developed by Thomas J. Peters and Robert H. Waterman, which was based on their book 'In Search of Excellence: Lessons from America's Best-Run Companies'. I learned a lot from this programme and the book, and I urge all entrepreneurs to find a copy of this book (and the programme) and lose yourself in it. It might be a little out of date now, but the fundamental lessons for business are timeless.

Before we start exploring what you can do to add value with your customers, I would like to suggest that you do a quick 'refresher' on the Measure chapter, with reference to the section on Products and Customers. In that chapter I talk about the importance of measurement, which implies that information must be available. Use this information as a weapon to seduce your customers and start the 'add value and innovation process'. Your customers will be impressed that you have statistics and that you are willing to share your information. They will also appreciate that your objective is to increase their sales opportunities.

exist for the customer

I 'stole' this heading from 'In Search of Excellence'. I believe that you start innovating with your customers when you bring your employees on board. All the 'I love customers' words are worthless unless you have the unconditional support of your employees.

How do you achieve this buy-in from your customers? A good start is to recruit the right people – those who share your values. We will talk about that in a later chapter. I would like to tell you how I worked on this issue - getting the employees to 'buy in'. My methods reflected my style of management, but they are not universal solutions. Learn from them and apply creative solutions to your own environment.

I used to have a 'customer lunch' every week. Preceding the lunch, the customer would be invited to 'tour' the various departments within the business. The customer was encouraged to ask questions of anybody. Our employees knew that they had to 'know their stuff', because their 'paymaster' was visiting. I invited an employee to attend the lunch. I also invited one of our employees to prepare the lunch for the day and host it on my behalf. These small, but important initiatives, helped to make every employee in the business feel important and needed. Their pride was more than visible. My customer guests were always very impressed – they were made to feel that they were our only customer. It might look as if we were showing off, but we were showing off our company, our products, our quality, our people and our commitment to our paymaster, and doing so with pride.

I am sure you have concluded from my story so far that I was a very process-oriented manager. In my early days at NGK Spark

Plugs, I realised that we had to influence the 'users' of our products, who were not our direct customers. I therefore implemented a system that ensured that our representatives called on direct and non-direct customers on a programmed basis. They presented a structured report on each call to the sales manager daily. That information allowed us to perform what I called the 'push – pull' process. In other words, we were able to inform distributors (direct customers) about sales opportunities at non-direct customers. This system allowed us to manage the product flow from factory to distributors to service installers. In doing so, we ensured that we took care of our retail customers, even though we did not deal with them directly. Our customers noticed the effect of our structured calling process. Their sales improved and we increased our market share. I accompanied our representatives on customer calls occasionally, but our non-customer facing employees also made customer calls. Again, this was noticed by our customers. More importantly, however, our non-customer facing employees became 'heroes' when they came back to the company and shared their 'war stories'.

Our employees became our ambassadors and that set the platform for us to start the process of innovating with our customers – they trusted us.

I often wish that I had been able to access today's technology in those 'historical' days!

innovate with customers

Our customer visits were not just calls. They were information gathering sessions. Someone once told me that God gave us two ears and one mouth and that we should use them in those proportions. Our calling system was structured to optimise the travel route and it considered a category assigned to a customer. The category was determined by the relative importance of the customer, which to a large extent determined the number and frequency of calls made on an annual basis. A record of each customer call was recorded on what we called 'The Customer Record', which was used to collect the following information:

contact details:
Contact details for existing and new personnel, which included phone numbers, birthdates, email addresses and social accounts.

call to action
List of unsolved issues for discussion, relating to current and prior calls.

performance review
Presents historical statistics on sales, revenue and account receivable balance for discussion.

opportunities
Lists discussion notes on marketing programs, incentives, new products, discontinued lines, pricing etc.

competitors
Lists notes on competitor activities.

Innovation
Lists discussion notes on our collective thoughts to improve sales volumes and supply chain efficiency.

get the order
A gentle reminder to the sales representative to 'get the order'.

This process had several purposes:

- gather market information
- share information with customer
- improve customer relationship
- improve representative productivity

The real purpose of this 'Customer Record', was to involve customers in eliminating any 'reasons' why they should not do business with us, but an important by-product was that most of our customers worked with us to make things better. This information further allowed us to identify those customers:

- who demanded the most up-to-date products and services and those most likely to already be trying things with top-flight competitors
- who were amenable to experimenting and evaluating new ideas

With these customers we were able to innovate and add real value to our business and theirs.

As I said earlier, I wish I had access to today's technology.

real and perceived service

I believe each of your customers should be made to feel that they are your only customer.

This is a very difficult task. It requires you, as leader, to take a personal interest in the quality of customer service being provided by your employees. You need to develop mechanisms to obtain quick and accurate feedback from your customers and you need to monitor that feedback. You need to set service goals and establish service measures within your business. You need to recognise top service performers from all departments, regularly and especially for those 'little things'. Those little things make a lasting impression on customers. Things like: returning a phone call quickly, saying 'thank you', smiling, listening, being honest, providing regular progress updates, etc.

Use your 'service orientated' culture to differentiate your business from your competitors.

I invite you to download an example of a customer service document.

download: customer touchpoints

This PDF document is a sample of an element in extracted from a customer care manual.

some things bother me

To improve efficiency, organisations resort to using technology. I get very frustrated when attempting to sort out a problem and I call a company, I am confronted by a 'call centre' and lots of options, which may include a request for me to complete a web form and describe my problem. I admit, I have encountered incredible service from some call centres, but that has been few and far between. All efforts to provide 'real and perceived service' can be destroyed in an instance when one cannot trust that the person in the call centre you are talking to, is not empowered to make decisions without additional superior consultations.

customers - in summary

Real value in your business is realised when:

- you and your employees accept that you exist for customers
- you innovate with your customers
- you create a culture of real and perceived service within your business

suppliers

Suppliers!

Remember, you are to your suppliers as your customers are to you. Well you should be!

If you expect loyalty from your customers, you should be loyal to your suppliers. I cannot dwell for long on this subject, but I suggest that you read the previous chapter again and put yourself in your customers' shoes.

the competitive spirit

I had never really thought about suppliers that way until I received a phone call from the personal assistant to the Chief Executive of the Toyota Marketing Co. South Africa. I was still working for NGK Spark Plug Co and was tipped off by the PA to prepare myself to say a few words at a gala dinner hosted by Toyota for their suppliers.

At the dinner, to my complete surprise, our company was announced as Toyota's Supplier of the Year! I was completely overwhelmed. My speech was unprepared for such an honour, and the accolades we received at the gala dinner left me feeling so immensely proud of our achievement that I could not sleep that night. However, it was nothing compared to the reaction when I presented the award to my employees the next morning. Our productivity that day was low, but we needed to celebrate and we did. We had been recognised as the best supplier to one of South Africa's most respected companies.

That award taught me two things:

- the award further opened the already competitive spirit within the company – clearly, my employees wanted that award again and they wanted to be recognised by our other customers

- I needed to do the same thing for my suppliers

In that year, we implemented our version of Supplier of the Year. In addition to the usual things, such as quality, delivery time, price and accounts presentation, we added an element on 'Innovation with NGK' with a significant weighting. We called on all our suppliers and explained our objectives and the judgement criteria. We had a mixed reaction. Companies who were eager to do more business with us took the competition seriously. Others who showed little enthusiasm gave us a good reason to invite prospective new suppliers to our family.

I therefore believe that you can add value to your business when you sign up suppliers who are keen to participate in your Suppliers of the Year competition. They obviously need to accept and understand the competition criteria. Take supplier meetings seriously, just as you take your customer meetings seriously. Introduce structure into meetings – reverse the customer record process I presented in the Customer chapter and keep a record of meetings – after all, you would need to do this to evaluate and judge their performance for the competition.

Oh, one way to add value to your business is offer extended financial terms. Just saying! One more thing – talk about ethics and values. Corruption must be avoided – get involved in contract re-negotiations, especially with high value deals.

suppliers - in summary

Real value in your business is realised when:

- you and your employees treat your suppliers as you would expect your customers to treat you
- nudge your suppliers to be part of your family and respect your values
- develop a code of conduct for suppliers and make this code available to all your employees as well

employees

I have made the point that employees are the most important asset in your business. When you invest in your employees, you add more importance to their lives, and in doing this, they will add more value to your business. Let us explore what you need to do to make this touch-point add real value to your business.

human resource policy

In a later chapter, I am going to spend some time talking about your new job as the leader of your business. You cannot create your asset of value by yourself. The most important part of your job will be to grow your business, and to do that, you will need to build up a good team of people to support you. They, in turn, will need to build up their teams. Your employment practices now need to be professionalised, which means you will need to develop a formal employment policy document. It is a document you should feel proud to present to a potential recruit. That potential recruit needs to decide if they are a 'cultural fit' and that they will abide by the 'company rules' before applying for a position in your business.

Your policy document will be successful when a new recruit, on employment, will place it in the 'bottom drawer' and never refer to it again.

What will be in this document?

context

In your policy document, you may want to add a short preamble to describe the context in which you operate. For example, in South Africa, we would need to pursue a human resources philosophy, mindful of our past, where discrimination and disparities in education, housing, property ownership and more, impacted negatively and traumatically on our people. It should be in our mind-set to attempt to try, in some small way, to redress the damage caused.

I cannot be prescriptive, in any way, in what you may want to say or not say. However, you will be employing people who should be treated with dignity and respect, and who should be given opportunities to achieve their dreams for themselves and their families.

I can, however, appeal to you to reflect on the high degree of inequality in the world. Your employment practices could, in a very small way, redress some inequality and poverty and provide dignity and opportunities to those people you employ.

philosophy

In another chapter, later in this book, I talk about the importance of reinforcing your philosophies, goals and ambitions into a formal mission statement.

Your values, as stated in your mission statement, should be included in this section of your policy document.

policies

In this section, you will provide a list, and supporting documents, outlining the employment rules within the business. These rules may include more than the following list:

- basic conditions of employment
- hours of work and overtime
- contribution to provident or pension funds
- contribution to medical insurance plans
- leave entitlement
- a template employment contract
- the grievance and disciplinary procedures
- health and safety rules
- advances and loans
- education advances
- training and development policy
- performance assessments

This list is not comprehensive. You will need to develop policies applicable to your business.

policy development strategy
I would like to suggest that you consider appointing a small multi-disciplinary committee to develop and maintain your human resource policy document. This committee can be appointed on a rotational basis, say annually. It would be required to consult widely with various work forums on issues affecting work conditions. They would present their recommendations for consideration to your executive management team, which team must always retain the right to manage and not be obliged to accede to any or every recommendation presented.

In this way, it can be arranged that your human resources policies will unfold as your journey progresses, and not be delivered all at once, as a big-bang event.

The committee can be charged with assisting in the communication and implementation of agreed policies.

recruit right

There is no perfect science to employee recruitment. We all get it wrong sometimes and when this happens, I recommend that you do not procrastinate on dealing with your mistake - make the change and cut your loss as quickly as possible.

The key question is: who is responsible for recruitment?

Sadly, I refer to my country again, where many laws were introduced to protect the general workforce from possible indiscriminate and unfair behaviour on the part of employers. A hiring mistake can therefore become very costly because of the onerous processes which need to be adhered to when de-hiring takes place, for whatever reason. Hiring has become a nightmare for line management, and as a result, they have outsourced this responsibility to the human resources department, who have positioned themselves as hiring experts. In many instances, these departments are usually very highly centrally controlled units, that enjoy calling the shots as to when, how, who, at what cost and under what terms, employees are hired.

These central structures have the effect of disintermediating what is intended to be an efficient connection between management and the general workforce. In the end, the workforce individuals lose out because they are 'grouped' into a workforce category which is unable to effectively present their abilities to the people that really count, their line management.

I do not believe that the human resource department should call the shots. The responsibility for employee recruitment and development should be that of line management. It should ideally be executed within a policy framework, developed in conjunction with the human resource department. Effecting efficiency and productivity is a line management responsibility, so it should be the line management that have the final say as to who and on what terms they hire 'their' employees.

Line managers must be made to take responsibility for all hiring and firing decisions, irrespective of any labour law complexity. Over time, they will learn from their mistakes, and more importantly, the grouped workforce mentality will evolve into that of a group of employees, who will be evaluated for their performance as individuals.

A word of warning – labour unions do not like this strategy.

purpose

When it comes to employees, a manager has only two duties:

- to ensure that each subordinate has a job which results in achieving a specific quota of measurable objectives
- to ensure that each employee successfully achieves their objectives

I am not a fan of job descriptions.

In the Planning Cycle chapter later in the book, I will discuss the process of creating an objective record sheet (ORS), which is used for planning projects in a financial period. This process is an ideal way to ensure that each employee is allocated specific quotas of measurable objectives. An ORS presents objectives for employees as follows:

effectiveness area
An effectiveness area is allocated.

objective
State what the employee is tasked to accomplish - each task must have a measurement method.

priority
Prioritise the task load.

measurement method
Provide a statement on how the task will be measured.

program of activities
Detail the activity steps required to achieve each objective.

date
Provide dates by when the activities are to start and finish.

actual performance
This space is available to record reviews on progress made in achieving the objectives.

objective record sheet
When each employee is served with their annual objective record sheet, there is no need for employee job descriptions. The ORS, together with the use of quality operational processes described in the Systems chapter, means that employees have jobs with measurable outputs, from which superior performance can be rewarded.

Each employee should participate in the development of their annual objective record sheet. These ORS's must be included in the various business units' operational plans.

When developing these ORS's, ensure that:

- employees are not overstressed by allocating them too many tasks
- tasks are simply presented
- targets are achievable
- the sum of employees' outputs must add up to the unit's target

download: ors

This PDF document is a sample of a completed objective record sheet and explanations of each of its elements.

development and training

In my career, I was blessed to be associated with organisations that valued the importance of training and developing their employees. I was a beneficiary of their wisdom. That wisdom was obviously transferred to me and I know that my management and employees were also beneficiaries of this wisdom.

When I became known for my enthusiasm regarding training, it seemed that I became the target for every training company's sales representatives in the world. There are so many training programmes available from so many training houses, and I was presented with a confusing array of choices. I decided instead to develop a training and development strategy, which I felt was applicable to the various industries I worked in. I categorised the training requirements into four categories, which are presented below. Managers were required to include a training schedule in their annual operational plans. Their training plans needed to list who, why, when, with whom and the cost. The training budget was guided by a pre-determined percentage of employment costs. Together with my team, we decided which vendors we would support – our goal was to achieve some degree of uniformity and continuity.

The training categories included:

management development

This type of programme was restricted to key managers and it involved issues around strategy, planning and the management of people. Managers attended these programmes on a rotational basis, usually annually. My thinking was that we would keep the team fresh with new ideas. Newly trained managers would report back and update those who had been previously trained. Lessons and practices learnt would obviously rub off on those who were yet to attend.

employee development

These types of programmes are referred to as soft skill programmes. In other words, technical or product related development training is not included. There are many types of programmes which can be included in this category, but I preferred to focus on five key issues:

problem solving

When people are taught to identify and solve problems, productivity and efficiency will improve. Applying some simple logic forces people to think about the way they can attend to issues without calling for immediate assistance. When this is done regularly, experience is developed and addressing issues becomes a way of life.

There are many programme vendors and problem solving is a key driver in all quality management programmes. They all teach the same basic functions, which include: identify the problem; identify where it did or did not occur; identify when it did or did not occur; identify why it did or did not occur. Once this is done, people are taught to list possible causes and to develop fixes and preventative actions.

behaviour management

When people are taught to deal with their colleagues in a way that recognises that they are 'different and not difficult', a lot of petty work issues can be solved quickly and easily. We have all experienced some form of disharmony between employee members. Using programmes that allow individuals to recognise the reason for differences in people goes a long way to improving office unity. It is not fool-proof, but I have witnessed huge shifts in behaviour, for the positive.

A particular vendor taught us to use a very simple technique to recognise behaviour characteristics in people we worked with or whom we met in a customer or a supplier interaction. There are many similar programmes available and I can only recommend that you experiment with a small group of your employees and judge for yourself as to how such a programme can add value.

customer care

I was always very focused on customer service in every business I managed, and the following downloadable file is an extract of what I called customer touch-points, which was used to evaluate ourselves. Feel free to adapt the file to suit your business.

corporate values

Later in the book, I talk about the importance of developing a formal mission statement for your business. Teaching and re-enforcing your corporate values system should be very high on your agenda. It was on mine.

I insisted that all my senior executives conducted small and regular workshops with employees to promote our values. They would conduct these workshops with employees that did not necessarily fall within their own operational units. This ensured diversity in the group and the executives got to 'know and get known'.

financial reports

I will be discussing communication and reward systems later. If you plan to implement an effective reward system, your employees will need to receive regular financial reports, which present actual performance measured against planned performance. This does not mean that employees need to be exposed to a full set of financial reports. Employees do, however, need to receive reports which pertain to their unit of activity, and they need to be trained to understand these reports. Your employees will then be in the loop, and in the long-run you will benefit from this training initiative.

skills

You would usually hire people because they have the skills you require to achieve your work objectives. That is why you pay them. I tended not to spend too much money in this area of development. I did not believe it was our purpose to pay for employees to acquire skills. We hired them for their skills. However, I would invest in skills training when and if resources were scarce or when issues of compliance demanded it. I was open to making 'educational loans' available to employees who met certain criteria.

product related

Products, processes and systems evolve continuously. Registering employees on scheduled 'knowledge upgrade' programmes is a very necessary business investment.

some words of concern

In many instances, I had to compete with the labour unions for the minds of some employees. I tried to ensure that all employees were not considered as just numbers within the organisation. I tried to differentiate 'us' from other companies by, amongst other things, developing a culture of continuous learning, which was recognised by employees. The money spent on performance-related learning and development was an investment, not a cost.

Today, traditional business is being disrupted by incredibly innovative technology that promises improved efficiency and reduced costs, but the side effect of technology is unfortunately to put jobs at risk. Labour unions will fight technology advancements to their last breath in order to protect jobs. In your new business, you will need to be mindful of what the future holds for you and the type of people you will need to hire in the future. You may need to ignore my foolish attitude of 'we hired them for their skills'. This will become a strategy issue which I will discuss later in the book.

Your business will evolve and the skill set requirements within your business will change. As a business leader, you must be flexible enough to renew your skill-set as and when required. You will face many road blocks in the form of legislation which tends to guarantee employment to certain people, and this type of guarantee will, to a large extent, be supported by labour union movements.

Spend money on training and development wisely, and make sure you align your 'investment' with your corporate goals.

performance review

As mentioned previously, I am not a fan of job descriptions, and neither am I a fan of formal performance reviews. My performance has never been formally reviewed and I have never reviewed any of my managers using a formal review tool.

I have learnt to do two things:

* catch someone doing something right
* help someone doing something poorly

To repeat what I said earlier about what your job as a manager entails:

* to ensure that each subordinate has a job which results in achieving a specific quota of measurable objectives

- to ensure that each employee successfully achieves their objectives

If you have set up a process of developing objective record sheets for all your employees, and they were included in that process, you will know very soon when an employee is not performing, and so will they. That is the time to talk. Engage in an informal chat and ask, 'how are things going?' Relate the feedback to the plans set and agreed upon. Listen to issues and provide ideas and opportunities for others to help. Your approach needs to be firm and business-like but empathetic. The outcome of the discussion should result in roadblocks being cleared to enable resumption of expected performance.

If the roadblocks have been cleared and poor performance is still an issue, make the change. Do not procrastinate!

Use this informal review process to recognise superior performance. Recognition motivates performance.

There are lots of books on performance management, and the formal review process does not have to be eliminated if it works for you or your business. It is your call.

rewards

I believe superior work performance should be rewarded. Furthermore, I believe reward systems should extend, if possible, to all employees in a business.

Reward systems need to be very well thought through, easy to understand and easy to implement. They do not necessarily need to be tied to employment contracts. I prefer flexibility in this regard, simply because things change and what is acceptable in one year may not be practical in the following year. It is more difficult to change the terms embedded in an employment contract than to review ad hoc incentive schemes on an annual basis.

I would like to share some thoughts on my experiences of implementing incentive schemes.

general principles

One of the most important lessons I learnt in implementing reward schemes was to link the incentive calculation to what I call the 'father and grandfather' results. What I tried to prevent was paying out a large incentive to an individual who had performed exceptionally well, but the department or company in which that individual was employed had incurred a loss. While the individual may have thought my thinking to be unfair, my logic was simple – owners should only be expected to pay incentives when there are profits available to do so. An individual incentive calculation should therefore be weighted, in some way, to take into account the performance to target of the 'father' and the 'grandfather' operations. For an individual, this may be a department and a company, or in the case of a branch, a region and a company, for example.

Another rule – make no exceptions. Very often, people will try to find a way to justify a reason for leniency. Ignore them with the comment: 'rules are rules'.

I have also found that making interim payments to participants may also attract problems. Early profits could be reversed by later losses. Be cautious. Consider paying out only a very small portion of the incentive on an interim basis.

innovation

Rewarding innovation, which leads to improved productivity, is a 'no-brainer'. I remember offering a productivity challenge to an administration department. The team worked together and presented me with a cost benefit analysis for introducing a software programme which saved time and money. The team was happy to accept the time saving in the form of 'time-off' for six months. Everybody won.

communication

In the chapter Keep in Touch, I introduced the 7-minute meeting. This form of communication is an excellent way to keep your employees informed. Technology is another way to improve communication. Imagine sharing key information as an app.

Whichever way you choose to do it, just do it. Employees do not like to be kept in the dark, and when they are kept in the loop, you will benefit.

I learnt one very special thing from the chairman of a company I worked for when he said to me:

> 'you write yourself apart and you talk yourself together'

Think about these words!

Should you find the need to discipline an employee – do not send a memo or an email. Talk and listen: face-to-face! Words on paper can never be withdrawn, but the spoken word can be explained.

labour unions

Management must accept that it is their responsibility to ensure that each employee is productive and becomes successful. This responsibility must not be abdicated and management must accept the fact that they will need to compete with labour union movements, which do not have the individual worker's interest at heart.

Early in my career, I naively found out that I was a member of an employee union. I thought nothing of it until it came to the annual salary review. I was awarded the same percentage adjustment as my colleagues. I objected as I felt that I worked harder and was more effective than my colleagues. I demanded that I be treated differently. I lost, of course, because the corporation had done a deal with the union and their hands were tied. I left the corporation – I wanted my efforts properly recognised and I did not want to be part of a collective.

in South Africa

In my view, the single biggest contributor to the increase in unemployment in South Africa is the rise in the power gifted to labour unions. The Government has used its alliance with labour union movements to partially finance the ruling party's (the ANC) political campaigns. In a cynical way, the workers are financing their own death. Let me explain. The more the ANC promotes their socialist ideologies, supported by the labour unions, the more South African industrialists become concerned. These industrialists introduce increasingly more efficient methods of production, or they simply outsource their production requirements to Chinese industrialists. Either way, they eliminate the need for South African labour.

The ANC missed a trick when they became South Africa's first democratic Government in 1994 by not encouraging industrialists to invest in South Africa and use the abundant labour force to create the start of a mini Korea. Imagine the wealth South Africa would have created by setting up factories and exporting its own beneficiated products to the world. The labour may have been cheaper at the time, but over time, people would have gained experience, skills and productivity. More importantly, however, the people would have had their dignity restored. They would have had jobs, earned some money, albeit a modest amount initially, and they would have been given the opportunity to set up a platform for the future for their children. Instead, the ANC co-opted unionists into Parliament, who proceeded to draw up labour laws which they believed would protect workers. However, their legislative efforts started the process of destroying jobs.

Something drastic needs to be done to neutralise the devastating effect the labour unions have had on the South African economy. The Minister of Education all but admitted that her department had lost control to unions on the appointment of key personnel at their schools. Union members were accused of taking bribes to facilitate key appointments, an accusation they vehemently denied. The unions do everything in their power to disrupt work operations, and when on strike, either protected or un-protected, they turn a blind eye to their members preventing non-union workers from exercising their constitutional right to work and earn a living. Their preventative actions often result in damage to property, injury and even death in many cases. The unions always claim to be innocent and I am yet to hear of any union official or member ever being held accountable for these dreadful deeds.

Why do I write this?

I do not like union movements, but I accept that they are part of our business lives. I believe that you, as an employer, need to compete with the labour unions for the hearts and minds of your employees. You need to create a working environment where your employees choose to have nothing to do with any labour movement.

environment

Do not ignore the importance that your work environment has on the productivity of your workforce. Your employees spend most of their awake time at work. They need to be comfortable; they need to have the right tools to perform their work; they need to feel secure; they need to enjoy being at work; they need to be respected and they need to be included. Your employees are people – treat them as if they were your family.

employees - in summary

Real value in your business is realised when you:

- define your rules of engagement
- recruit the right people
- define what is expected of your employees
- train and develop your employees

- reward your employees for excellent work
- communicate effectively with your employees
- compete for hearts and minds of all your employees
- treat your employees with dignity and respect

infrastructure

Remember my definition of infrastructure. Infrastructure is the term used to describe the assets within your business from with you derive income. It includes buildings, vehicles, plant and equipment, furniture and fittings, computer equipment and so on. These assets may be owned or leased.

costs

I worked in the motor retail industry for a period. The motor retail industry is very tough and competitive. I was really bothered about the demands the motor manufacturers placed on us, their franchisees, in the guise of 'dealer standards'. I understood the need for them to have their brand image presented in a consistent manner across all their franchise dealers, but I never understood and appreciated the expense which we were expected to incur so that they could achieve their objectives. On the first day of every month, we knew we had to sell a defined number of units at the 'right' margin, just to pay the rent.

It was scary!

While I accept and encourage that infrastructure can and should be used to elevate brand awareness, may I suggest a word of caution: do not go overboard. Every dollar spent on infrastructure incurs additional 'down-the-line' costs in the form of depreciation and maintenance.

When purchasing infrastructure, consider three things:

- its ability to improve productivity
- its ability to improve efficiency
- its cost effectiveness

Here is a small but important example: although an office chair must be functional, i.e. something to sit on, it should also contribute to improving productivity. No business wants their employees suffering from back pain caused by a 'functional' asset. Choose the chair wisely – you get what you pay for!

I believe that a 'cost benefit analysis' should be done for every infrastructure asset purchased. You need to evaluate the cost of owning an asset as opposed to leasing it. The correct decision, one way or the other, will add value to your business, especially if its actual lifespan outlasts its anticipated lifespan, without unnecessary increases in maintenance and operating costs.

Think about how new environment innovations can assist in reducing costs, especially in your buildings. Deploying solar technology, if possible, creates a great opportunity to reduce energy costs, but do the cost benefit calculation.

download: cba
This Microsoft Excel spreadsheet is designed as an interactive teaching tool. It allows for the evaluation of savings efficiency when considering the purchase of assets used in the production of income.

image

Do not underestimate the value of your image in your marketplace. Your assets are an effective way to promote brand awareness. Branding on company vehicles, for example, can be an effective way to promote image. However, the bad driving behaviour of the driver can quickly destroy that image. Think about that!

Make a point of using branding on your assets effectively. Buildings and vehicles are a very cost-effective way to add additional value to your business.

infrastructure - in summary

Real value in your business is realised when:

- you purchase assets that will cost-effectively improve productivity and efficiency

- you evaluate your purchase by doing a cost benefit analysis
- you use your assets to enhance your image, but do not go overboard with unnecessary expense

systems

By the time you read this, what I am about to say on adding value to your business through systems is going to be out of date. Fortunately, or unfortunately, this is a fact. The Internet has changed our lives and has created countless opportunities for us to improve efficiency and productivity.

The software industry reacts to innovation from the computer hardware manufacturers, who in turn react to customer demands from the software industry. A good example is the invention of the tablet computer. Tablets stimulated the market for the development of applications, known as 'apps'. The apps, in turn, stimulated the demand for tablet computers and smart phones. The use of apps on tablets, computers and smart phones has changed the way business people want to trade and monitor the performance of their businesses.

The only thing I can say for sure is that no matter which system you choose today, it is going to be out of date tomorrow.

selection strategy

You have managed your business using systems that have been appropriate for your needs and have chosen those that are affordable and practical.

System innovation is the standout business touch-point where you can dramatically improve efficiencies within your business, and at the same time gain a real competitive advantage. The implementation of systems and their upgrades can be traumatic, however, if not done properly. Apart from the implementation of minor systems, I am yet to experience an implementation or an upgrade which has been delivered on time and within budget. This usually scares managers to the point where they continually postpone the upgrading of any system.

At the end of this chapter, I offer a general 'case study' where the successful implementation of a supply chain strategy improves efficiencies, reduces costs and increases market opportunities. While I am cautioning you on the problems you may encounter, I am also appealing to you to step back and review how systems are deployed within your business. It is essential to keep investigating how modern systems can positively impact on your business processes and market opportunities.

It is also a worthwhile exercise to take some time out to think about what you will require in terms of upgrading the systems within your business. Systems advisors are taught to understand the users' requirements, but very often the users do not know exactly what they require. They also do not know what is available to improve efficiency. Systems houses often develop their systems to meet 'a-one-size-fits-all', and while this approach can apply, you may find that you have a unique requirement. This means that you must accept a compromise or wait for an expensive modification to the system. Whatever the situation, you need to sit down and define your requirements very carefully.

ease of use

I have to say that most modern systems are easy to use. You still, however, may need training, especially for new employees. The full range of features within a system are often not effectively used, and even a small amount of formal training can go a long way to ensuring that the 'right people' within your business can work at optimal efficiency.

ease of implementation

It does not help if the system is easy to use but difficult to implement and expensive to maintain. Take this into consideration when choosing a system.

development speed

Business is dynamic and you need to choose a system that is easy to adapt to your changing needs, for the least cost. Systems have evolved to a point where one can deploy a rapid-development implementation, which is important when one develops a system from 'scratch'. This means that the system can be used while development is still in progress, in the same way that various apps which you purchase are regularly upgraded.

support

Obviously, you do not necessarily want to be the guinea pig when your business depends on a system – there is a time to be 'bleeding edge' and a time to adopt a slightly more conservative approach. However, you may not want to miss out on something which could offer you a very dynamic and competitive advantage. You can choose to factor in a risk element, in which case you will need to have a high degree of confidence in the developers, preferably gained through evaluating their delivery success on previous projects.

It is a good idea to ensure that any new system can be supported by more than one vendor.

cost effectiveness

You need to evaluate the cost very carefully when purchasing a new system, especially what is termed 'total cost of ownership'. In addition to the initial software costs, you will need to determine its implementation costs, on-going operating costs, support costs, licence costs and the costs to develop unique features which may be required. These costs must be weighed up against the actual deliverables of the system. Too often, systems are chosen because of their initial cost, but changes need to be made when the system is unable to deliver important requirements. The real cost of an inexpensive system becomes apparent if and when costly changes are required.

scale

Ensure that the system you choose is more than capable of meeting your current demands. It should also be capable of rapidly scaling up to meet anticipated future demands at minimal cost.

migration ability

The ideal situation would be to have installed systems within your business which allow data migration to other 'open' systems without too much programming effort. Any new system deployed should have the same characteristics. This gives you options to migrate your data to systems which offer greater efficiencies at reduced costs.

dynamic information consolidation

Rapidly changing business environments lead to demands for various types of business information on an 'on-demand' basis. This information may need to be extracted from various disparate systems located in operations around the world. The system you consider will need to have the capability to seamlessly transfer any information across to some form of information consolidation software.

systems

There are many systems available to you from many software vendors. Do not be the person who puts a smile on every software representative's face. They will tell you that their product will solve all your problems, but in my experience, most of the systems I have purchased have not been able to do everything it was claimed they could do, including making coffee!

I would like to suggest that you focus on a few systems where you believe you can improve efficiencies and gain a competitive advantage. Consider the implementation of the following systems:

accounting and administration

Accounting and administration will be the most important systems investment you will need to make in your business. Almost any other system you install will be dependent on information from an efficient accounting and administration system. In the Keep Score chapter we talked about the need to produce accurate financial information on demand. This system will need to measure performance by department, branch, region, sub-divisions, divisions, and by group. It must be able to measure performance against the financial plan and the previous financial period.

budgeting and forecasting

A budgeting system is necessary to assist with the production of your annual financial plan. It must be able to produce information as structured in the accounting and administration system. In addition to a budgeting system, you may consider introducing a hi-level modelling tool, which allows you to evaluate new business opportunities or the quality of the forecast earnings and resultant cash flow when business conditions change.

human resources

The administration of employees in and out of service is becoming an important legal requirement. Human resources systems are therefore evolving into very comprehensive programmes which record employee information and history relating to: service, leave, remuneration, promotion, performance assessment, training and development, and even disciplinary history. These systems are also used as communication tools, where employees can interrogate personal information via the internet.

customer relationship management (CRM)

In a previous chapter, I talked about the importance of innovating with customers. You can only do that when you get to know your customers well. You need to ensure that they deal with your business because of your products and the service you provide, and not because of a person within your business. The implementation of an effective customer relationship management system helps you solve that issue and much more.

Systems used today are very effective and may draw on cloud technology to allow you to retrieve customer information, interactions and much more on any device and on an on-demand basis.

This type of system is only effective, however, when you, as its champion, drive the programme. I have seen very poor results – not because the system was bad, but because it was not driven by top management. Select your system carefully and drive its implementation yourself. Timing is also important. Do not implement it when you are starting your business. You need a stable operating environment and then you will get better employee involvement, especially if the system is easy to use and information seamlessly integrates into your financial system. In my experience, customer-facing employees do not like doing administrative functions, so do not over burden them with these tasks.

business intelligence

I have talked a lot about the need to have information on the operations of your business at your fingertips. This information needs to be both accurate and dynamic and it must be presented to you in a simple and uncluttered form. There are many systems available on the market. My experience, however, is that these systems offer 'everything' when you only need to focus on a few 'top-line' issues.

My advice is to introduce this type of system slowly and deliberately. Using web technology, it is possible to have an app developed, which collects information from your various systems and presents it to you via a computer, tablet or a mobile device. I would have such a system 'purposely' developed rather than purchasing an 'off-the-shelf' system.

quality

I thought a lot about introducing the management of quality into this segment. Being a quality orientated business does not mean that you have to manufacture something. Being quality orientated means that you are orientated towards managing your business with well-defined operational processes, driven by well thought through policies.

If there are systems available for managing the quality processes within a business, it would be worth finding out whether there is one to suit your particular business or one which can be customised to your requirements.

In previous chapters I have talked about my successes in embedding a quality culture within the organisations. This culture system may be seen, by many, as a costly exercise. My experience, however, is that the benefits derived by inculcating this culture into your business far outweigh the cost of non-conformance to systems. Little things count, like quantifying the value of 'customer returns' and working out how much these returns can be reduced. When people are taught the value of 'doing things right the first time', they will soon see the benefits of observing this principle.

The advantage of introducing a quality culture is that there is no need for a 'big bang' implementation. Implementation can be introduced at a pace that suits the business, which could be done in such a way as to show 'quick and easy' wins.

resource strategy

Up until recently, there was always a big debate as to whether computer infrastructure and its support should be an 'in-house function' or should be outsourced to various service providers.

Today, the reliability and speed of the internet provides you with many more service options from which to choose. Cloud computing has added a new dimension to the problem of keeping up to date with technology. I cannot offer any specific advice, except that you should evaluate all options and select a solution or combination of solutions which suits your requirements and budget.

implementation strategy

As I have said, I am yet to experience a system implementation or a system upgrade which was delivered on time and within budget. These projects can cause all kinds of problems, including a loss of faith in technology. My advice:

- plan well
- prepare well
- have a backup plan
- do not be a guinea pig
- unless you really need it, do not buy it and implement it
- unless you really need to, do not upgrade
- only introduce technology when it adds real value
- do not do anything technology related when you do not have adequate resources

a case study – supply chain system

Now for some innovation.

I refer again to the Financial Viability chapter, where I discussed the management of a business' net assets. Lower net assets result in reduced interest charges, and astute management of your business' inventory levels will contribute to a reduction in the net assets.

In attempting to reduce inventory levels, one must not lose sight of some very important factors: service levels – inventory levels cannot be at levels where sales may be lost; shrinkage – of fast moving, high value and perishable items must be well controlled; and cost of orders – the cost of placing orders must be balanced against the frequency of placing orders.

Innovative systems and good management will go some way to achieving these objectives. However, inventory levels can be further reduced if customers' sales forecasts are dynamically aggregated and presented electronically to suppliers. This means that the flow of goods from suppliers to customers could become a continuous process, resulting in the reduction of inventory levels in the business, as well as those of the suppliers and customers.

In order to achieve the required reduction in inventory levels, the co-operation of both customers and suppliers is needed, but this could be achieved through the implementation of a supply chain system with seamless integration.

This concept is further enhanced when logistics providers are also integrated into the supply chain systems. Customers' goods could be delivered directly from suppliers.

Supply chain systems already enable this, thus adding value to all participants.

systems - in summary

Your systems strategy can be the touch-point that engenders a culture of innovation in your business. Use systems to improve efficiencies, reduce costs and create competitive advantages. Invest wisely, but remember, poor implementation can also set you back very quickly and at great cost.

leader

You have now reached the point where you need to stop working in your business and start working on your business.

Your new job will be about adding value to your business in a very focused way. This is how it is done.

grow the business

scenarios

Assume you own a profitable engineering business which manufactures various components used in the motor industry. Your sales are dependent on the growth of that industry. If vehicle sales decrease, the sales of your components will decrease, and your profits will probably decrease at a greater rate. You may also be at risk from a change in technology or from competitive situations, where the products you manufacture are substituted by another competitor who is able to produce them more economically.

In another scenario, you may own a profitable retail operation supplying hardware and building supplies to your local community. One day, without any warning, a national building supplies chain decides to open a new branch very close to your community. They have a strong brand, as well as the financial resources to price their products very competitively, and this puts your business seriously at risk.

In both cases, your business would be in trouble if you had not been thinking about growing your business or even diversifying it. The point I am making is that there is no certainty in business. Be prepared for the unexpected.

strategy

In your quest to create an asset of value, you need to do whatever is necessary to protect your business against uncertainty. This will include applying your mind to developing a strategy on how you will protect and grow the future profits of your business. In the manufacturing scenario, your strategy may include diversification, and in the retail scenario, it may include opening additional branches or adding a service component to your operation to counter unwelcome, but inevitable, competition.

I would like to suggest that you refer back to the Financial Viability chapter to understand the importance of generating cash, particularly in the startup years, to assist in the funding of your growth strategy.

build the team

You cannot do everything yourself. You need to build a team of people around you that will allow you to implement your growth strategy. I was given this advice: 'Never work for anyone who is not smarter than you, and never hire anyone who is not smarter than you'. That advice is not always practical to implement but looking for 'smart' qualities in the people you hire is a very sound concept. Hiring smart people will help you to achieve your goals, but make sure that they buy into your values. This is a priority.

trust

You are going to have to trust people. Building trust is easy to say, but not easy to do. You need to start by being honest, fair, beyond reproach and trustworthy. You are going to have to go more than halfway when there is doubt. You will need to regularly assess how things are going with people who are not a part of your 'inner circle'.

Trust is not something you start with; trust is something you end up with. Trust is generally built during a process of many interventions. In building trust, you need to focus on the problems that separate you from the people you need to trust, and not focus simply on building good relationships. When you solve problems, and get some real issues out of the way, you build up a solid base on which to place your trust in people.

Trusting people is not easy, but it is necessary.

standards
When building that team of people around you, it is essential to set high standards with specific, but not unrealistic, goals and objectives. You need to communicate these expectations clearly and the rationale behind them. Do not apologise if they are difficult. Listen to the objections of those who resist and consider their concerns carefully. In planning what to do, you need to ensure that each team member has the necessary core competencies and capabilities to accept the responsibility of achieving their set objectives.

participation
Participation in projects cannot be voluntary – it must be mandatory. If, for example, improving quality in your organisation is essential to gaining a competitive advantage, then participating in the quality improvement program needs to be compulsory. You may, however, consider giving people time to adapt to changes and allow voluntary participation. If the implementation of a program is critical to the success of the organisation, their mandatory participation must be non-negotiable.

organisation structure
It is time to experiment. Your objective is to improve communication and management's effectiveness. You may, for example, have added several branches to your business operation, which run autonomously, meaning that all operational functions, such as accounting, hiring and procurement, are performed at branch level. To balance costs and management efficiency, you may want to try some experimentation. Centralising the accounting functions may reduce costs, but centralising the procurement functions may impair effectiveness, which could be detrimental to the business.

The chief executive of a very large successful South African industrial group once said to me: 'We could probably save R50m a year if we centralise certain functions, but we make all our profits because we don't'. Over time, you will need to experiment on structures that yield the best results for your organisation in terms of costs and effectiveness.

Be careful not to create a structure around one particular person, because this may not work when that person is no longer with you. I firmly believe that structured lines of authority, where managers are given the autonomy to run their operations without too much interference, are the most effective. People perform much better when they are given responsibility and are involved in goal-setting.

delegate
Delegating authority can be very daunting.

When I was a young manager, the facilitator called me aside during a team workshop and asked me if I knew what I was doing to my team. He had observed that I was the guy who was first in the office and the guy who switched off the lights at night. I knew virtually every movement of each manager. He pointed out to me that I was in the process of creating human robots, who simply waited for instructions from me. I was stifling their freedom to perform effectively, and more importantly, I created a lot more work for myself.

I needed that honest observation. I called in my team and informed them that I would be trying very hard to change my 'controlling and somewhat autocratic behaviour', and I needed their help and support to do so. Over time, I worked very hard to adjust my behaviour, but I concluded that I had hired the wrong people. I did not have confidence in their abilities to independently carry out tasks. When delegating autonomy, you need to let people know exactly what their freedom and authority limits are, and you need to assure yourself that they have the necessary skills and tools to accept that responsibility.

Granting autonomy does not mean abdication; on the contrary, it means harder work. Your people need your wisdom and support, which means you need to keep in touch with them - you cannot leave them without direction and support. When granting autonomy, focus initially on your direct team members' work detail. Eventually, you will see that autonomy travels downwards to the people who really do the work. You may need to explore and remove any unnecessary constraints that hinder a successful delegation exercise.

reward

Your reward system is critical for encouraging appropriate behaviour. It must be simple, easy to understand and consistent in its implementation. You need to ensure that your reward and recognition systems reinforce behaviour you deem critical for success. Regular communication is necessary, and it must be honest. People need to know why they are being rewarded or punished.

Both success and the behaviour should be rewarded psychologically and financially. Tie your reward system as close as possible to activities over which your people have direct control and minimise those activities over which they have no control. Sharing wealth derived from excellent financial results, for example, is a very good strategy to create long-term value for your business.

information

If you really want people to care about your plans and goals, let them in on them. People do not care about things they do not know about.

Share information! Information is power. It is the kind of power that must be shared if you want people to know what they must do to add value. If you treat people like outsiders and do not let them know what is going on within the business, they will act like outsiders. Sharing information is not giving up control: it is one of the most important things you can do to change the fortunes of your business. When people feel they are a part of your plans, they will treat your business as if it were their own.

do not procrastinate

Sometimes things do not work out as planned. You may find that a team member is not an 'ideal fit' in a team and is, in fact, a hindrance to the effectiveness of its performance. Situations like this must not be tolerated for too long. Make a change and cut your costs as soon as you realise things are not working out. Remember, your first loss is usually your best loss.

gender diversification

A final thought.

In building your team do not be afraid to bring diversification to your team in terms of gender and race.

protect your values

In the next chapter I am going to talk, in detail, about the formalisation of your mission statement. Your behaviour up to this point will be reflected in that document. More importantly, however, your behaviour will have been noticed and ideally emulated by all your employees. A small thing like picking up a little piece of paper from the floor will be noticed. An important thing will also be noticed, such as returning a customer's phone call, as promised, and telling them the truth about why their delivery will be late.

You have been building your values and one day they will be formalised into your mission statement. That should not matter, however, as one of your most important jobs will be to protect your values at all costs. Your value system is your unique signature, which you lend to your employees to utilise on your behalf.

Protect those values at all costs.

MBWA

I previously talked about how I was influenced by a programme called 'Towards Excellence', developed by Thomas J. Peters and Robert H. Waterman. This programme emphasises the use of MBWA.

MBWA is an acronym for 'managing by wondering around'.

This is a very powerful way to see, hear and listen. Do not underestimate the power of your presence. A simple personal greeting to a woman on a production line means so much to her. A call on a customer, with a representative, has a double benefit – the customer feels important and the representative is motivated to 'show off' his boss. It is a time to obtain first-hand feedback as to how things are 'really' working on the ground. A word of warning, however. Do not use this time to give instructions. You may be the boss, but that does not give you the right to interfere in the line management's authority. A quiet discussion with the line manager on your observations will be far more beneficial.

Introduce MBWA into your new job and you will add real value to your business.

leader - in summary

Your new job is to work on your business and not in your business. The first thing to concentrate on is starting the process of growing your business. Secondly, you will surround yourself with a strong management team, and thirdly, you will work hard to protect the values on which you founded your business. Practice MBWA and add real value to your business.

part 6

professionalise

Why professionalise? You have created your asset of value, but your work does not end there.

Allow me to use an analogy:

You have baked a cake and now you need to top it with beautiful icing. The quality and presentation of that icing will attract a buyer with discerning taste, who is prepared to pay a premium for its quality.

That is why you need to professionalise, and the next three chapters we will explore how you ice your cake.

statements of intent

I first became aware of the concept of a mission statement in the early part of my career, soon after I joined a well-respected South African motor retail group. I embraced the process of developing the mission statement with great enthusiasm.

Why?

I applied for a position in this motor group which I believed I was well qualified for. My CV secured me an interview, and after the first interview, I was informed that I had been placed on a 'shortlist'. What I did not know at the time is that I was the only candidate on the so-called shortlist. I was interviewed by the chief executive of the group and, after meeting me, he evidently developed another agenda. After a few more entertaining discussions, I remember asking him 'so, are you going to hire me or not?' The reply was an emphatic 'yes'.

In these discussions, I felt there was something special about this man, and about his attitude and pride towards his organisation. The interview process was less about my skills and ability to do the job – it was more about how I would fit into the organisation and accept its culture. I later discovered that the chief executive had been leading the process of formalising the organisation's mission statement. He could see that I was a 'fit' and I was offered the job, which marked the beginning of a new direction in my career.

During your journey up to this point, you have slowly embedded your personal values and created a special culture within your business. You will have surrounded yourself with employees who support and buy in to that culture. Now it is time to formalise those values, and you will do this through two distinct statements - a mission statement and a manifesto.

mission statement

What is a mission statement?

A mission statement defines an entity's reason for existence. It embodies its philosophies, goals and ambitions. Its members are its intended audience. It is a statement to its members of their focus, and it is also a subtle message to them on what must not be done. In simple terms, and by way of an example, if you are a specialist manufacturer and distributor of fast moving consumer goods, do not attempt to become a specialist component manufacturer and distributor of hi-tech medical equipment, simply because an opportunity is presented to you.

Developing the mission statement, as I have discovered, is not easy. The mission statement is a short but powerful paragraph encapsulating your reason for being, your guiding principles, a brief description of your industry and an outline of the business you are in. It also describes exactly what you do, outlines your products, states who your customers will be and describes how you get your products to market.

When I joined the motor group, I was charged with the responsibility of developing the company's mission statement. The chief executive believed that I would be in the best position, as an 'outsider', to co-ordinate its development.

I set up a small team to assist me with this project, and we set about our work as follows:

define the business

I was the best person to write the definition statement. I thought I had a clear idea of what a motor retail business entailed. It was surely about selling new and used vehicles, servicing customers' vehicles and providing the parts and related items associated with servicing vehicles?

It turned out to be about all of the above, plus a lot more. I discovered a vehicle rental unit, a safari unit, a finance unit and a paint and panel shop, as well as other 'associate' companies all trading under the management of the motor retail group. This made my first task difficult. How was I going to encapsulate the essence of this business in a short but powerful paragraph?

I politely presented my new boss with my dilemma and was cheeky enough to ask whether the 'associated' non-motor retail businesses contributed fairly to the overall group's contribution? It turned out that they did not, so the first decision was made – I would start by focusing on the motor retail business first and we would consider the other businesses at a later stage. I argued for focus.

As a matter of interest, a few years later, all non-motor retail businesses were either disposed of or transferred to other divisions, where they could flourish under specialist management.

a working document

Writing the 'working document' also presented challenges. South Africa is a very culturally diverse country. The group portrayed South Africa and its various languages and cultural groups, so the challenge was to write the 'draft' mission statement in a way that it would be easily understood by all. Do not underestimate this task. The language needs to be simple and precise and should not give rise to any misunderstandings whatsoever.

We made the mistake of writing it without consulting the 'people on the ground'. We used words that were not necessarily understood by all, without explanation. The test is to have a prospective new employee read the document and understand it without an explanation, or with very little explanation.

buy-in

We undertook this part of the project very well, but in fairness, the company culture was, to a large extent, in place and ready to embrace some formality. This was to the credit of the chief executive, who had been with the company for a while and had been working very hard to inculcate and embed its unique culture and supporting values. We arranged many small workshops, comprising of natural working teams. The working document was handed out to each employee. Its purpose was explained and discussion was encouraged. The teams were given time to review the document, to 'live' it and to test its applicability in the workplace. Follow-up workshops were arranged to review comments from the many teams. We discovered that there was very little disagreement on the presentation of our reason for being, our guiding principles, our industry, our business, what we do, our products, our customers and how we get our products to market. We did, however, encounter the need to extend the debate on clarifying our core values. We found that we needed to identify fewer values – values that were most central to our organisation and its long-term market goals. Besides the fact that these values needed to be relevant and meaningful, they needed to be well articulated.

Values need to be perceived as more than just 'words on paper'. They need to be clear, focused and factual statements, which are easily understood and 'naturally' implementable. Misleading statements will not fly.

We considered proposed amendments and presented them to the company's executive committee and board. The final mission statement had been developed.

This process, I must warn, was not a quick one. I cannot remember exactly how long it took, but I do recall that I needed patience. My advice, if you adopt this process, is to take your time and get it done properly.

launch

We chose what I called a 'soft launch'. We took 'framed' presentations of our Mission Statement back to those teams that had been charged with the responsibility to review the originally proposed document. We requested that these framed presentations be displayed in prominent customer facing areas.

This proved to be a mistake.

Later in my career, I chose not to present the company's mission statement to anyone other than my employees. I learnt that it did not matter how good our intentions were towards our customers, we could still make mistakes, albeit unintentionally.

I remember an incident where a customer deliberately misled one of my employees on an issue. After investigating the issue, I chose to support my employee. The customer was appalled and became publicly abusive towards the company. The customer played on a value in our mission statement, which read: 'We treat our Employees with dignity and respect'. The customer accused us of not treating the customer with dignity and respect.

I know the incident, like most, was blown out of proportion, but I realised then that there was no need for us to advertise our objectives and values to the world. Instead, the world should experience our values without the need for us to advertise them. I learnt that a mission statement was not meant to be a customer-facing presentation. As stated in the definition above, the mission statement is meant to serve the members of the organisation and not its general stakeholders.

evaluation and training

A mission statement is a living document so one needs to do two things:

- translate the values into mundane actions – the acid test is its application into everyday behaviour, particularly the values
- reassess these values at regular intervals because things change

The major thrust of values is not likely to change, but interpretations may shift over time. Make sure you can demonstrate changes.

what a mission statement may say

Presented below are several element statements from mission statements I have seen:

profile
We are part of the ABC Group and provide a full range of services to companies within the specific industry.

purpose
We provide XYZ solutions designed to enhance customer productivity. By introducing modern methods of doing business, we enable these businesses to improve profitability by opening new markets at reduced operating costs.

vision
Our business goal is to become the best at what we do and be recognised as such by our customers.

Our organisational goal is to become the home for highly talented and energetic young professionals in our industry.

objectives
Philosophical objective:

• every startup entrepreneur in South Africa must become a customer for one of our products

In our first year of operation:

• launch the following app suites: trading, manufacturing and services

In our first year of operation we will achieve the following:

• revenue - $1,000,000
• tax profit - $300,000

- ROA – 25.00%
- debt / equity - .30

values

The values that underpin everything we do are:

- we develop high quality apps, which are affordable and easy to use
- without prejudicing the need to invest in excellent people, systems and innovation, we pledge frugality so as not to waste money on unnecessary expenditure

a manifesto

What is a manifesto?

A manifesto tells everyone who you are, what you believe in and why you are prepared to invest in a cause. It is a public declaration of intent.

I had not come across the concept of a manifesto during my career, which meant that I had never written one. My son, George, introduced me to this concept, and he argued that the concept of presenting a mission statement was old-fashioned. Because a mission statement had always worked for me in the past, I was not about to give up on the concept too readily. However, on doing further research on a manifesto, I realised that there was a place for both statements in an organisation. I wish I had thought of the concept myself many years ago.

To sum up the fundamental difference between the two, a mission statement is inwardly focused and a manifesto is outwardly focused.

Apple Inc.

In researching the applicability of a manifesto for an organisation, I was referred to Apple Inc. Tim Cook, as CEO, introduced the 'Apple Way' six months before Steve Jobs passed away. The following declaration left employees and investors believing that Apple could go on without Steve Jobs. This is what it said:

> 'There is an extraordinary breadth and depth in our more than 35,000 employees, who are all wicked smart. And that's in all areas of the company from engineering to marketing, operations and sales and all the rest. The values of our company are all extremely well entrenched.
>
> We believe that we're on the face of the earth to make great products and that's not changing. We're constantly focusing on innovating. We believe in the simple, not the complex.
>
> We believe we need to own and control the primary technologies behind the products that we make and participate only in markets where we can make a significant contribution.
>
> We believe in saying no to thousands of projects so that we can focus on the few that are meaningful to us. We believe in deep collaboration and cross pollination in order to innovate in a way others cannot.
>
> We don't settle for anything other than excellence in any group in the company, and we have the self-honesty to admit when we're wrong and the courage to change.'

The message was clear, regardless of who was in which job. Those values are so embedded in the Apple company that it should always do extremely well.

Tim Cook's manifesto speech illustrated the following six key elements:

emotional principles

- Apple's compelling purpose is about making awesome products

core values

- the manifesto includes core values such as innovation, collaboration and excellence, and it even admits error

truth
- the manifesto is authentic and touches emotions

business to personal link
- the manifesto did not do this simply because, in their world, tech and home life are intertwined – a manifesto should link the two

inclusive
- the manifesto touches and moves everybody

differentiation
- the manifesto emphasises differentiation, in simple terms

So, unlike a mission statement, a manifesto will have as its objective, an ignition to act. It must be framed in emotionally charged language to influence the future.

statement of intent - in summary

Start the professionalisation of your business by developing your mission statement. A manifesto can follow when your business has established itself as a successful, well recognised operation.

planning cycle

I am sure you have heard the terms 'budget time', 'year-end' and 'audit time'. I call them trigger points.

As a startup entrepreneur, focused on getting your business running successfully, you did not worry too much about these trigger points. In fact, apart from 'financial year end', these terms were foreign to you. However, as your business grows, you will face a variety of new challenges. You are no longer thinking of day-to-day activities – you are thinking of expansion. Expansion may come in the form of new outlets, new products, additional productive employees and acquisitions. Expansion requires additional resources in the form of infrastructure, inventory, receivables, equipment and employees.

The triggers are the final, but one, step in the development of the systems, which support the sustainable growth of your business. We will discuss the 'but one' in the next chapter. You have set up systems around the management of your touch-points, and now it is time to set up your annual planning calendar.

the trigger points

As I said, I call them the trigger points and I list them as follows:

- innovation laboratory
- preparation checklist
- planning workshop
- budget
- operational plan
- financial year-end
- audit signoff
- celebrate

The timing of the trigger points within your business depends on two factors – the complexity of your business or group, and the date of your business's financial year-end. I would always like to see the completion of the budgets as close to the year-end as possible. This allows for year-end forecasts to be more accurate and, therefore, the budget base for the new year becomes more realistic. I cannot provide any formula for this – you will have to judge or set the length of time it will take to complete each trigger point properly, and then work backwards from the financial year-end date.

The complexity of your business will depend on many factors – for example, the number of branches. When your business gets bigger, or becomes part of a larger group, you may have to consider regions, sub-divisions, divisions and groups. In other words, the 'deeper' the structure, the more time it will take to complete all the triggers. Your budgeting and planning systems will also have an impact on the timing.

be prepared

These processes consume time, and generally the people that need to work on these trigger points also have their 'day jobs'. Attending meetings, carrying out research and working on the trigger points take additional time. Do not be surprised when tempers fray. Be understanding!

Let us discuss what needs to be done for each trigger point.

innovation laboratory

I discussed the concept of an innovation laboratory in the planning section of this book. I arranged many innovation laboratories during a financial period. On an informal basis, I would invite a cross section of employees from various departments, to occasionally 'shoot the breeze' with me. On occasions I would include a guest. In these meetings I encouraged out-of-the box thinking. No minutes were taken and no expectations were raised. We simply talked about 'crazy' ideas, which could impact our business into the future.

In addition to these meetings, I would attend conferences from which I thought I could learn more about innovation in one form or another. I would try to talk to other business leaders and share ideas.

I would bank ideas for discussion in the annual planning workshops.

preparation checklist

Before every annual planning workshop, I would send out an informal checklist to each manager attending the workshop. Its intention was to provoke discussion within their branches or companies and present ideas on how to improve future financial performance. In this way, we offered all employees the opportunity to participate in the business's annual planning process.

I did not expect long detailed reports. I wanted a 'one pager' outlining recommendations on what was required to get their operations from their present situation to a more desired place.

The checklist below is not a universal document – it served my purpose for the motor retail business I managed, but I am sure you will add or deduct elements to accommodate your business if required.

the business
Update its overview and history.

business systems
Review applicability and effectiveness of all business support software and hardware.

business facilities
Review state of facilities - changes proposed and costs.

budgeting
Is budgeting software adequate?

benchmarking

Does the business engage in any benchmarking activities? Who were the participants in those activities, and what was the result? Do managers participate and do they understand the standards? Do they understand the relevant operating ratios and will training assist their understanding?

business reporting

Are business reporting systems adequate? Is a DOC system in place, who gets it and when? What happens when things are out of line? How frequently do meetings take place and at what levels? Are meetings productive? Are the meetings formal?

business controls

Are business controls in place? How frequently are reconciliations checked and who does them? What audit functions are in place? Have there been any problems in the past with regards to fraud and stock losses? What security systems are in place?

communication

Are communication processes effective? How are employees, customers and suppliers kept informed?

customer relationship marketing

Is a customer relationships program in place?

customer service index

Is a customer service index (CSI) system in place? Are there incentives in place to reward performance and is training required to improve their standing? Is CSI taken seriously?

employee retention

Is employee culture aligned with the company's values? Are employees changes frequent, and if so, why? Are their employees willing to accept change? Are there any 'Holy Cows'?

employee development
Does the company have a culture of learning? What policies do they have in place to develop the employees, particularly in the areas of management development and technical skills within the business?

franchisor requirements
Is the business adhering to any franchisors' standards? Does the business meet those standards, and what are the reasons for non-compliance? List any areas of non-compliance.

franchise and territory
Are there any threats or opportunities within the franchise territory?

labour unions
Are labour unions constructively involved in the business?

locations and franchise
List details of locations, types of businesses at the various locations and employee numbers. What changes are envisaged?

management
List details of management and number of people employed. What changes are envisaged.

management style
Is the company's management style in line with values?

mission statement
Is the mission statement still relevant? What needs amending?

organisation structure
Detail the organisation structure. What changes are envisaged?

products and market performance
Review brand performance. How are competitors rated?

relationships
Present a general relationship overview on customers, suppliers and employees.

remuneration and performance systems
Are remuneration and incentive systems in line with policy? Are they appropriate?

statutory information
Is there compliance in all statutory issues?

planning workshop

The objective of the planning workshop is to provide a blueprint for the development of the organisation's budget and the operational plan for the new year.

I regarded the planning workshop as the most important trigger in the planning cycle. We were well into the current financial period so we knew how well or how poorly we were performing. I used this meeting as an opportunity to socialise with my team and their families. While we worked, our 'significant others' and the children were out at play, enjoying the ambiance of the chosen retreat venue. A planning workshop is the ideal opportunity to take a few days and get away from the business.

I invited my executive team to the workshop. I would also include managers who were being developed for future promotion. On some occasions, I asked an external consultant to facilitate the workshop. I did this because I did not want to be seen to dominate the process and 'get my way'. An external face can bring a good balance to brain-storming and problem-solving sessions.

programme
Managing the workshop programme can also be a challenge and that is another very good reason to invite a facilitator. Make sure that all the workshop participants are well briefed on the workshop's agenda and encourage preparation. In my experience, discussions can become prolonged and heated, and preparation work helps participants to stay focused on the programme.

Let us discuss the process I adopted for my planning workshops. While it worked for me, I am sure you will develop your own process over time. My programme agenda consisted of the following sessions:

- executive expectations
- team process
- team partnership
- statements of intent
- burning issues
- object record sheet

The output of this workshop will be a blueprint for the preparation of the budget and the operational plan.

Some advice - have a scribe attend the workshop. In this way all important decisions will be captured into pre-prepared template documents, which can be made available to the delegates almost immediately afterwards.

executive expectations

I treated this short session as an 'ice-breaker'. I invited the 'significant others' to attend. My logic – they are silent partners in our success and they deserved some recognition, albeit in a small way. In this session, I reminded the team about the objectives of the workshop. I briefly reviewed the businesses' performance to date and presented a scenario on the prospects going forward. I also outlined my expectations of the workshop.

team process

In this session, we explored the dynamics of the team. We reviewed each team member's performance and their contribution to the overall team's performance. Each member's performance was 'peer' reviewed. The member being reviewed was not allowed to enter any discussion whatsoever. However, they were able to interrogate the critique with two statements: 'tell me more' and 'give me a for instance'. This ensured that supported facts needed to be presented to support a critique. I encouraged frank engagement but I insisted that we played the ball and not the man. The atmosphere became quite volatile at times.

We used this time to review the appropriateness of the organisation's structure.

team partnership

In this session, we reviewed the various characteristics of the individual team members. Before the workshop, each member's management style was evaluated using a specific psychometric tool. This session was fun and we needed that, especially after the frequent tension of the previous session.

I am a strong believer in these types of tools, provided that the behaviour lessons are applied consistently throughout the organisation. I have experienced a great deal of success in developing teamwork within my companies using this method. The success was more prolific in the sales departments. We all learned that 'people are not difficult - they are different'. In fact, I referred to this session as the one where 'we bring our unique gifts to the team'.

statements of intent

This session is devoted to reviewing the company's mission statement. I took this very seriously. I needed to understand that our purpose, objectives and values were still appropriate and that our people were still 'captured' by our culture. I always wanted to know how we could strengthen our value system. We updated the objectives annually and presented them to the company at our annual celebration event.

I was never involved in the company manifesto, but you may consider it as part of this session.

burning issues

This session has its origins in the preparation checklist. The objective of this session is to identify issues that need urgent attention and areas where support is needed. We also used this time to table strategic issues which needed attention at some time in the future, but which were not operational in nature. Strategic issues are addressed in another forum, which I will discuss in the final chapter.

I developed what I thought was a unique process to identify the most important issues that needed attention. It may not be unique, but it worked for me.

The issue sponsor (delegate) was given two minutes per issue to highlight an issue in terms of:

- impact – cost to the company
- impact – on other departments or processes
- frequency – how often it occurred
- location – where it occurred and where it did not occur
- possible solution – and at what cost

These issues should be supported by a cost benefit analysis study if possible.

download: cba

This Microsoft Excel spreadsheet is designed as an interactive teaching tool. It allows for the evaluation of savings efficiency when considering the purchase of assets used in the production of income.

The team was given another two minutes to ask any clarifying questions.

The issues were presented in rotation. In other words, each delegate presented one issue at a time. These issues were written up on butcher paper and pinned to any available visible wall.

At the end of the process, the delegates were allowed some time to study the walls and make their own assessments on the importance of each issue.

Each delegate was required to list, in order of importance, the top five issues which should be selected for attention. The votes on these short-listed items were counted and the final top five items were presented for attention.

I facilitated a discussion on the issues presented with the objective of seeking consensus from the team on what needed to be done. The list stood, but on a few occasions, we intervened to deal with specific issues and the solution may have resulted in an additional issue being added to the list or one being replaced.

Over the many years of applying this process, I made two observations. Firstly, there were many 'oh dear' moments when team members realised that their actions, or inactions, may have caused inconvenience to a fellow team member. Secondly, for some reason, the items that were not selected for attention were resolved in one way or another.

In my early career, my enthusiasm used to get the better of me and I listed every issue for attention. My boss and mentor called me in and gave me some very good advice, which was to do fewer things and to do them very well. His advice was sound. I realised I was not Superman. I learnt from that advice and I started learning the lesson of 'focus'. Five items seemed a good number.

objective record sheet (ORS)

This is the final session of the workshop. The burning issues are on the table and they need to be addressed. I designed a simple form, which I called the 'objective record sheet', which I used to record the details of each issue, which was now termed as a project. The form allows each project to be presented in a structured format, which includes the following:

effectiveness area

Identify each effectiveness area in no more than four words.

objective

State as clearly as possible what you plan to accomplish. Each objective must have a measurement method.

priority

Prioritise each objective. Several objectives may have the same priority.

measurement method

Provide a clear statement on the method used to measure the objective.

program of activities

These are specific activities undertaken as steps towards achieving the objectives. These are inputs, which are not substitutes for, or supplementary to, the objectives. These inputs assist with planning.

date

Provide dates by when each activity is to start and finish.

actual performance

Detail the achievements as measured by the measurement method, in the time section. Do not measure the program of activities. In addition, include a statement of whether the objective was overachieved, just achieved, or underachieved. If under-achieved, a clear and accurate explanation of the reasons why should be given.

This form should be used when projects are being developed by 'down-the-line' teams.

download: ors

This PDF document is a sample of a completed objective record sheet and explanations of each of its elements.

budget

In the chapter Keep Score, I talked about the importance of keeping accurate and up-to-date books. In another chapter, Systems, I talked about the need to introduce systems which improve efficiency and productivity.

In my experience, the budget process usually goes smoothly when the books are up-to-date and an efficient budget system is deployed. However, the process needs to be well defined and well communicated.

Let me present some thoughts on how to make the budget process efficient and successful.

top down forecasts

I developed a modelling tool to support the type of business I managed at the time. I used Microsoft Excel simply because I was very familiar with its functionality. This tool was hi-level in nature and it didn't 'circumcise mosquitoes' to the extent that a budget model would. It allowed me to evaluate the quality of the forecast earnings and resultant cash flow if I changed assumptions affecting key business elements, such as contribution, expenses, asset levels and funding strategies.

I used the information from the income statement, balance sheet, cash flow statement and key ratios to present guidelines for the preparation of the budgets.

These guidelines were communicated to each divisional manager and their respective budget officer. The communication included timelines for review and consolidation, as well as common assumptions such as inflation rates and funding cost rates. It would also include various expense parameters such as group administration costs.

I would use my forecasts as a benchmark against the consolidated budget results.

I have included a sample hi-level forecast model which can be readily adapted.

download: hi-level forecast

This Microsoft Excel spreadsheet is designed as an interactive teaching tool. It is an example of what a hi-level forecast model may look like and achieve, in terms of forecasting earnings of a business for the balance of a current financial period and five years beyond. This tool works best when data is entered systematically, in the cells from the top of the spreadsheet. As each element is completed, evaluate the effect of the assumptions in the income statement, balance sheet, cash flow and the key ratio reports.

budget tool

I insisted that only one type of budget modelling tool was to be used throughout the various operating divisions. Its structure needed to be compatible with the accounting systems so that base data costs, such as employment costs, fixed assets and structured loans could be exchanged seamlessly.

bottom up involvement

You may remember my discussion on the allocation of responsibilities in the chapter on Employees. The allocation of responsibility requires that each employee ought to have some say in the budget. This process is not too onerous if the monthly reporting processes include sharing the financial results with all employees. The employees will know how the business unit evaluates their contribution. For example, if a sales unit consists of 10 people and their annual aggregate revenue contribution is $10,000,000, and revenue levels are projected to increase by 10.00%, each sales person should agree to their personal targets being increased by the same rate. There needs to be some involvement and consultation with the sales team to test the budget assumptions.

The process of setting targets can become controversial, however, especially if employees are incentivised to exceed budgeted levels. What may happen is that those employees will argue for lower targets in the knowledge that they will earn larger incentives because the targets are easily achievable. The counter to this is the setting of targets at levels which are unachievable. The consequence of this will be demotivated employees. The trick, as a leader, is to push for superior performance without being unrealistic. Make sure that the incentive systems are structured towards achieving qualitative results and not only quantitative results.

It is a mistake not to include the employees in the budget process.

comparisons

An important component of a budget is the forecast results of the current financial period. I included an 'adjusted mechanistic forecast' feature in the budget system. This meant, for example, that if the budget was being prepared from a base month which was nine months into the financial period, the year-end forecast formula would be: cumulative value to that point divided by nine multiplied by twelve. The formula would also include an adjustment field so that the budget officer is able to adjust the calculated forecast by a value that results in a realistic forecast.

In the end, you really want to have a realistic current-year forecast evaluated against the new year's budget forecast. You need to do this line-by-line, if necessary. To use my words, 'circumcise mosquitoes'.

review

The review process is the most stressful time for the budget officer. The budget officer is the person standing between the bosses and the employees, who are responsible for achieving the numbers. The bosses want more and the employees have all the reasons why they cannot achieve the bosses' demands. The budget officers find themselves frequently adjusting the numbers. A well-structured timetable and the co-operation of all parties in adhering to these timelines makes the budget officers' lives easier.

The technology available today can make life easier for all. Budget systems can be migrated to cloud-based technology. This means, for example, that adjustments at a branch level can be automatically updated for regional or divisional consolidation, and these results can immediately be made available to authorised budget reviewers. Coupled with electronic messaging systems, the budget review process will be completed in less time and with reduced stress.

A tip for the employees: motivate your forecast position with solid facts. Bosses will listen to reason.

finalisation

Once the review process is complete, the budget officer needs to complete two final steps:

- budget breakdown
- inclusion into the financial system

The budget breakdown step needs to be done so that the numbers are included in the various operational plans.

The budget officer must ensure that the numbers are transferred into the financial accounting system. These numbers need to be broken down by department at operating level.

operational plan

Having done all this work, it would seem pointless if the outcomes were not crafted into a formal document and made available to your team members. In my early career and under the mentorship of 'that' motor dealer chief executive, I was 'instructed' to write a very formal plan, which he would also present to his board. I had no option but to oblige, but I found the task time-consuming and I felt out of my comfort zone.

This is what it contained:

executive summary

The executive summary consisted of a summary of the company's mission statement, a review of the past year's performance and the key objectives for the new financial year.

the industry

I wrote an analysis of the industry in which we operated, explaining the competitive environment and how we planned to exploit opportunities and deal with any threats that may challenge us.

products

I presented a synopsis of our various products and how they solved customers' problems. I talked about the relationship we had developed with our suppliers and provided statistics on our market share position. I presented some thoughts on challenges we faced and how we planned to deal with them.

the market and marketing strategy

I described the competitive environment in which we operated and presented our perceptions of our competitors' strengths and weaknesses. I set out our key objectives in terms of unit sales, margins and contributions, and I provided details on how we planned to achieve these objectives and at what cost.

operations

I described our business environment, including the production operations and capacity, our branch network and our supply chain. I described how we did business from our various facilities. I provided my perceptions on their suitability and our plans to improve, expand or close wasteful operations.

management and employees

I described the organisation structure and provided details of key management. This included our plans for training and development. I was especially focused on length of service and the age demographics of the organisation. While I did not publicise my plans for succession, those plans were very much alive and shared with my boss and key executives within the organisation.

capital expenditure

I always provided a schedule of capital expenditure, details of costs, the reason for their purchase and how we planned to finance each asset.

implementation schedule

In this section, I presented a copy of each objective record sheet (ORS), which we created in the planning workshop. I also presented a summary schedule for purposes of brevity.

observations

Later in my career, I re-evaluated the value of the time I spent writing this plan. In my view, the most important part of the plan was the presentation of the ORS. I recognised the document's value but I found that many managers, including myself, were not 'wordsmiths' and this part of the planning process was a big frustration for us.

I had a long discussion with my boss about my observations and we reached a compromise. A divisional executive would write an impactful executive summary not exceeding two pages, which could be presented to the board. Their managers would get on with the job of managing their businesses.

I believed that there was more value in reviewing the plan, and I will discuss this process in the next chapter.

Although it was not easy, I have to say that the process of compiling the plan did add value. I acquired an intimate understanding of the business, including its problems and our plans to sort them out. I used to say that because I wrote the document, I was able to 'put it in the drawer'. I knew what was needed to be done. I can therefore recommend developing the complete package, but you can decide for yourself whether it is necessary.

financial year-end

This part of the planning cycle belongs to the financial teams, but if you remember my chapter called Keep Score, I encouraged keeping the books accurate and up to date. If this is done properly, there should be no need for much extra work. There may be a scheduled 'full stock-take', but even this could be advanced to the month prior to the year-end.

The accountants know what needs to be done so it is best to stay away from them for a little while.

audit signoff

I welcomed the work performed by the external auditors. While I knew it was our responsibility to present true and fair accounts, it was always re-assuring to have the auditor's signoff on our work. I participated in their 'audit findings' discussion and took their findings and opinions seriously. I did not always agree, however, to implement their recommendations if I thought they did not add value and our risk of non-implementation was minimal.

Once the audit was complete, I celebrated that milestone by having a special lunch with the finance department and the auditors. It was a tradition that they paid for the lunch on alternate years.

The finance department deserved to be recognised and rewarded.

celebrate

Jack Welch, the legendary former chairman and chief executive of the GE Corporation, makes a point of the importance of celebrating success in his book entitled 'Jack', which is an excellent read.

Once the hard work is done, it is time to celebrate the success of the year's achievements. I used this opportunity to present various awards, including recognising 'long-service' and 'star performers' to those very special people who produced excellent results.

I also used this occasion to review the past year's performance and present our plans for the new year.

planning cycle - in summary

You are in the process of professionalising your business and this is probably the most important step to making your business become less dependent on your expertise. You have appointed competent management and you are getting closer to that next step in creating your asset of value.

review and react

There would be no point in developing the operational plan if it is not reviewed regularly and diligently.

planning board

In my days, I created a 'war room' where the details of our plans were displayed for everyone to see. There were many planning boards, each of which displayed the plans of a department or a specific project. Our progress was charted on these boards to present high visibility of our progress. My assistant was charged with the responsibility of preparing a structured meeting schedule for all projects recorded in the operational plan, and she did this in conjunction with the various project co-ordinators. My assistant also co-ordinated all the meetings and updated the planning boards. In other words, the relevant team members were informed of meetings and attendance records were maintained. I was kept in the loop on all projects in an informal way, and I occasionally invited myself to meetings.

Today, there is innovative technology available which can streamline the process of scheduling meetings, but I doubt that technology can replace the team gathering to get the job done.

meetings

In the chapter Keep in Touch, I presented some tips for running a successful meeting. I am not one for lots of meetings, but meetings are essential for communicating, planning, reviewing and decision-making. Review those tips again, because you as a leader will spend a lot of your time in meetings, so making them productive is very important.

Let us spend a little time reviewing the type of meetings that could take place within your business.

7-minute meeting

The contents and objectives of this meeting was discussed in the Keep in Touch chapter. The 7-minute meeting is designed to eliminate unnecessary dialogue, which can sometimes lead to deviations and off the point discussions. It is efficient and achieves a daily structured two-way communication.

departmental review

This meeting will occur on a regular basis and at the discretion of the departmental head. It will be informal in nature, and its purpose is likely to be one of communication.

performance review

This type of meeting will occur on a frequent basis. Its purpose is to measure performance in the production and sales environments. It is likely to be informal in nature with a strong emphasis on obtaining information regarding opportunities and threats. Actual performance will be measured against targets. Deviations should be assessed and tested quickly with a view to initiating corrective action where appropriate.

The information will flow through to the finance and project teams if necessary, where concomitant decisions may need implementation. For example, if sales volumes declined suddenly, it would have a knock-on effect on production and procurement requirements. It may also have an impact on a related project, where increased production capacity was being planned.

executive committee (EXCO)

This type of meeting would take place monthly. Its purpose would be to review the performance of the business as a team. It is likely to be very structured in nature, which means that formal minutes or notes would be taken and presented to the team soon after the meeting for further action on decisions taken at the meeting.

board meetings

You have reached the point where governance of your company is becoming very important. Although you may still be the only shareholder or even a majority shareholder, you would be wise to have considered the appointment of non-executive directors, including an independent chairperson to your board. As the business grows, the role of these directors becomes more important in managing the governance of your company and determining its strategy. Board meetings would be scheduled on a quarterly basis and will be formal in nature. This means that minutes will be taken and presented to the members soon after the meeting for further action on decisions taken at the meeting.

board committee meetings

Independent board members will be appointed for their specific skills and they would be given the additional responsibility of chairing various governance sub-committees, such as audit, remuneration and legal. These meetings would be scheduled on an ad hoc basis and will also be formal in nature. That means that minutes will be taken and presented to the members soon after the meeting for further action on decisions taken at the meeting.

ops planning

These meetings will occur as per the prepared schedule. The purpose of the meetings is to monitor the progress of the projects as set out in the operational plan. The meetings are not meant to be too formal, but progress will be updated on the various OCR sheets. I would be kept informed on progress in an informal way and more formally through the EXCO meetings.

some thoughts

Things go wrong! Things change!

because it is planned, does not mean it is on

The best advice I can give about planning is: do not cast your plans in concrete. The purpose of these meetings is not only to review progress; it is also to react if things are not going to plan. Reacting means making tough decisions quickly. The motor industry has a phrase: 'your first loss is your best loss'. If it means that you need to close an operation, do it swiftly. Do not be sentimental. I have seen businesses land themselves in real trouble because sentiment called the shots. A delay in reacting may strain your financial resources and that could do more harm to your business in the long term.

Change may also mean doing things a different way due to new technology. Go to your board and motivate the need to change if you find better methodologies. If your proposal makes economic sense, the board will evaluate it favourably. I am making this point because the board will have pre-allocated financial resources to projects and would have to make alternative arrangements to accommodate changes.

watch those mavericks
Let us talk about the allocation of financial resources to projects within a group of companies. My very first management appointment was as the manager of a building supplies branch in the 'sticks', as we say in South Africa. This rurally positioned branch was one of many in the group, and the group owned a diversified portfolio of businesses. The branch was not performing to its target.

I was excited by the challenge, and very soon the branch's fortunes had turned for the better. I managed to accelerate its performance well beyond budgeted levels. One day, I received a phone call from the group's chief executive advising me that he had planned a trip to my branch and he wanted me to join him for dinner. I naturally assumed that I was going to be recognised for my achievements.

Not so! The chief executive was a Chartered Accountant, a numbers man, and he ran the group under very tight financial disciplines. My operation was a drop in the ocean, in the context of its size within the group. Over dinner, I was given a lesson in fiscal management. His point was that unless my growth was generating cash, I was a burden to the group. It was a very tough lesson in cash flow management for me. I needed to 'stick to the plan'. I understood his point, which was that with a few more 'mavericks' like me (his words), the group could get into trouble because of commitments made to shareholders and funders.

I regarded that dinner as a very good business lesson.

My point is that plans may need to be made in the context of a 'big picture strategy'. When performance is reviewed, focus not only on the poor performers - watch out for those mavericks too.

misconduct

In the chapter Keep Score, I talked about the importance of audit and verification. You will be a very lucky manager if you never encounter an incident of theft within your company. It will happen, and it has happened to me. It is a gut-wrenching feeling when you must face that person, fire that person and report that person to the authorities, especially after you have placed your trust in that person.

I can only advise that you place high importance on verifications. Make it a culture within your meetings to talk about the need to remove temptation from 'everyone'. In a group which I worked in, the group chief executive would 'drop in' at a branch unexpectedly and ask to see the monthly reconciliation files. His actions and tactics were well known throughout the group, and while it was not a fool-proof system, it was nevertheless a very strong deterrent against financial misconduct.

My final point on this matter: deal with any incident swiftly, decisively and ruthlessly.

review and react - in summary

There is real value in reviewing performance. Make it part of your culture. Instil structure into all meetings and make a point of reacting quickly, decisively and without sentiment.

Remember: your first loss is your best loss.

part 7

asset of value

'If your dreams don't scare you, they are too small'

Sir Richard Branson

Let us explore your options.

what now?

Well that is up to you!

what you have

You have a professionally managed business or group of businesses.

You, or you and your partners, have worked very hard to get your startup dream to this point. You have sacrificed many things along the way and hopefully, you have also enjoyed some fruits along the way.

What does this mean?

It means you have grown your business either organically or by acquisition, or both. You have invested, re-invested, restructured and you have built a brand which has become admired and respected. You have been an innovative supplier of products and services to a loyal customer base, who have come to depend on your existence. You have been a loyal supporter to suppliers, who have also valued your business as their customer. You have invested in infrastructure and you have developed systems and processes, which have allowed the business to flourish. You have borrowed money from financial institutions and you have repaid loans advanced. You have paid taxes on profits generated, which means you have contributed to the economy and the social upliftment of your community and country.

Most importantly, you have employed people who have become loyal employees. These people have been developed and trained to become professional custodians of the other touch-points. You have been able to go on holiday, attend to some personal issues and even play that game of golf now and again, in the knowledge that your 'back is covered'. Your business has grown more profitably because your employees have added value.

You have created your asset of value.

I remember talking to my CEO, who had won an award for being the 'Best Entrepreneur in the World'. He had a strategy for buying majority stakes in companies which was based on a very simple philosophy: he sought businesses which were run by owners who were entrepreneurial by nature, and who were able to add greater value to his group if empowered with resources in the form of finance and access to additional market opportunities. He recognised their hard work and was happy to pay what he called 'a fair value' for their asset of value.

The asset of value which you have created may now be a very important asset for someone else.

options

If your asset of value becomes an asset in the eyes of a potential buyer, you now have options.

These options will depend on your personal objectives. In the chapter, Business Plan, you were asked to state what they were. These objectives may well have changed during your business journey, and you have every right to change them. Your decision could be influenced by many factors:

- age - your age will have a bearing on any decision you make: if you are still in your prime, your youth will allow you to continue managing the business and conversely; your mature age may encourage you to step aside from onerous executive responsibilities
- health - your health may hinder your ability to manage your business and that will affect your decision
- succession - the absence of a viable succession plan will affect your decision
- enthusiasm - you may be a serial entrepreneur and get bored once you have achieved a specific objective, which will influence your decision

sell all

You could sell your entire shareholding to partners, if you had any, or you could sell to an outside investor. Selling to a partner has advantages, particularly for your employees and, of course, they are familiar with the business and its culture, assuming they were actively involved in it. The disadvantage, however, is that you may not realise the optimal value of your shares, compared with the option of selling them to an outside investor. You could be released from all executive responsibilities soon after the sale, depending on conditions set in the sale agreement.

sell some shares

If you chose to sell a minority share-holding, it would be a strategic move, on your part, to wean in a new shareholder or partner. This would allow that partner to become familiar with your business so that they can prepare themselves for some future executive responsibilities. When the time is right, you may find yourself selling your entire holding to that new partner.

If you chose to sell a minority share-holding, it may be a strategic move on the part of the new partner to acquire the entire share-holding in the longer term. They would use your presence to effect a smooth transition into their systems and procedures.

Both scenarios would allow you to realise some value for yourself in the short term. Both scenarios are very often traumatic for your employees. The transition process needs to be well managed. Your employees need to realise that the new shareholders will create new opportunities for the business, which will be in their interest.

In both cases, make sure you have a well-crafted shareholders' agreement so that you can buy back the shares at a pre-determined value should things not work out. The agreement should also include the terms and formula regarding the amount you will be paid when you sell the balance of your share-holding.

value enhancement

You may not want to sell your business. You may want to continue managing your business, especially if there are growth opportunities which would add more value to your business.

A solution is to raise capital through what is called an initial public offer (IPO), where you offer shares in your company to institutional investors who, in turn, may sell them to the private shareholders on a securities exchange. In this way you transform your privately-owned company into a public listed company. By doing this, you allow the market to put a value on your asset of value.

There are advantages and disadvantages in this transformation.

One disadvantage is that you serve a much larger and more discerning ownership base. Decisions you make will therefore always need to be made in the best interest of all the shareholders. While you may have followed that thought process in the past, you and your partners, if you had any, were the only shareholders. Decision-making was simple – now it is not. You are now subjected to a whole new realm of governance issues, even though you may have been preparing for this. You will be subjected to many more statutory reporting protocols. Your behaviour and that of your company, at large, will be intensely scrutinised, be it good or bad. The process is also very expensive, but you will be advised on that when preparing a listing prospectus.

An initial public offer (IPO) will result in a dilution in your ownership quantum in your company. The value of your share-holding will now be determined by the market, which will be in your hands. The market places a value on the company, based on its perception of your management's ability to produce a future income stream, in order to yield their anticipated earning hurdle rate.

So, while you may have reduced your share-holding in the company, the value of your reduced share-holding may have increased beyond what you may have thought it to be worth originally.

download: valuator

This Microsoft Excel spreadsheet is designed as an interactive teaching tool. It teaches the basics of doing a high-level valuation of a business. It is not a comprehensive evaluation tool, but it does provide five basic measurement criteria for evaluation purposes.

consider

When presented with these options, you will need to consider issues regarding your management and your succession plans within the business. A buyer wants to know that the business is not too dependent on you for its survival. You will need to demonstrate that you have built up a management team that can run the business in your absence.

The employment of family in a business may also be of concern to a prospective buyer. You will need to demonstrate that family are worthy appointments and that nepotism is not a culture within the business. Family members should be treated in the same way as any other employees.

valuation

The value of a company is stated in a line on the company's balance sheet called shareholders' equity. The shareholders' equity is the owners' net worth in the company, should it be liquidated. This net worth includes the initial capital, accrued undistributed profits and loans due to the shareholders. The value of a single share, therefore, is that value divided by the number of shares in issue.

If you were to attempt to raise funds from a financial institution, that institution would pay a great deal of attention to this value to secure its loan advance. In addition, however, it would want to be assured that your business was generating profits and free cash flow to be able to repay their loan, with interest.

Potential buyers of your business, on the other hand, would look at your business from another perspective. They are interested in the income stream your business can generate for them in the future. They set themselves a target hurdle rate to buy assets, which can yield a specific return on their investment over a specified time. They would do what is called a 'due diligence' exercise on your business to evaluate its potential to achieve those earnings flows. They would discount those earnings by a rate which included inflation and risk. The calculated value would be the amount they would be prepared to offer you for your business.

You would have to evaluate that amount against your expectations, and the bargaining will begin until both parties are happy.

professional assistance

I suggest that you seek the assistance of professional advisors to guide you through this process. Do not attempt to do it yourself.

Finally, make sure that you have a good legal advisor. Do not release those shares unless there is a water-tight agreement in place and the money is in the bank.

what now? in summary

You have created your asset of value and now you have choices to either cash in or enhance its value even further. However, just because you have reached this point on the value curve, it does not mean you can sit back and relax. You have reached a decision 'crossroad'.

in conclusion

I wrote this book with two types of entrepreneurs in mind:

- those who are thinking about starting their own business and
- those who want to turn their existing business into more than 'just a business'

Developing a new business or improving an existing one is a step-by-step process. It can be adapted to the implementation of any project, simply by following the five fundamental steps below:

- research
- plan
- start
- touch-points
- professionalise

Once you have launched your business, it is essential to 'stay ahead of the curve' by adding these two ingredients:

- innovation
- technology

Many startup businesses fail and I have shared my personal insights in the hope of reducing the rate of failures.

More importantly, however, I would like to think that my contribution will assist all new and existing entrepreneurs to realise their dreams of creating an asset of value.

******

toolbox

In many instances, I could not present an effective graphic to support a point I was trying to make, so I have created a series of support files which can be downloaded from the BizzBean website. These files are Microsoft Excel and Adobe PDF files. Please download the files and modify them to suit your own unique requirements.

access to the files

To access these files, kindly register at www.bizzbean.com.

applications

The files referenced in the book are available from the BizzBean website for download. The applications are listed in alphabetic order and reference the relevant chapter.

The blue cells in the spreadsheets are used for data entry, while the other cells have been password protected, with the password set at **BizzBean**. The Excel comments feature is used to explain the information required in each key cell.

assets

chapter: keep score

This Microsoft Excel spreadsheet is designed as an interactive teaching tool.

It has two components: a simple asset register and a lease asset register. It can work for a small business, but it will need to have rows inserted to accommodate additional asset items. This is easily done.

The fixed assets component aggregates the monthly depreciation and the balance sheet value of each fixed asset item, while the leased asset component aggregates the monthly lease values of each leased item.

bcg

chapter: products

This is a PDF graphic illustration, which explains the theory of the BCG Model.

bizzplan template

chapter: business plan

This PDF document shows what the BizzPlan business plan template looks like and the type of information it presents. It is a checklist to guide you through the development of your own business plan, if you chose not to use the BizzPlan app.

breakeven calculator

chapter: financial viability
This Microsoft Excel spreadsheet is designed as an interactive teaching tool.

It teaches how to calculate the breakeven point in a trading business. It provides opportunities to simulate 'what if' situations.

cash flow

chapter: call to action
This Microsoft Excel spreadsheet is designed as an interactive teaching tool.

It can be used to forecast daily cash balances in a small trading business. Although simple, it is effective.

contribution mix

chapter: financial viability
This Microsoft Excel spreadsheet is designed as an interactive teaching tool.

It allows the creation of various product mix scenarios and demonstrates how changes to unit sales volumes, unit selling prices and unit cost prices will affect the aggregate gross profit contribution in a business.

cba

chapter: infrastructure, planning cycle
This Microsoft Excel spreadsheet is designed as an interactive teaching tool.

It allows for the evaluation of savings efficiency when considering the purchase of assets used in the production of income.

customer analysis

chapter: measure

This Microsoft Excel spreadsheet is designed as an interactive teaching tool.

It is an example on how product contribution can be analysed for each customer. It can be adapted to accommodate many additional records, which ideally can be imported from an accounting system.

customer touch-points

chapter: customers, employees

This PDF document is a sample of an element in extracted from a customer care manual.

definitions

This is a PDF document, which contains a list of accounting definitions, designed to improve understanding of terms used in various financial reports.

doc

chapter: call to action, keep score

This Microsoft Excel spreadsheet is designed as an interactive teaching tool.

It is a simple example of a daily operating control sheet (DOC). It compares monthly cumulative results against forecasts for: revenue, gross profit, expenses, net operating profit, inventory, receivables, payables, net assets and the bank balance.

dynamics

chapter: financial viability

This Microsoft Excel spreadsheet is designed as an interactive teaching tool.

It allows for the evaluation of changes to various business elements such as: contribution, expenses, interest and taxation, working capital and funding, on the profitability of a business. Real learning value is derived when used in conjunction with other downloadable spreadsheets such as the funding calculator, net asset management and working capital.

funding calculator

chapter: financial viability

This Microsoft Excel spreadsheet is designed as an interactive teaching tool.

It allows for the evaluation of changes to various balance sheet elements such as: total assets, non-interest-bearing debt and interest-bearing debt. It shows how interest paid is affected by the structure of debt and equity on a business' balance sheet.

hi-level forecast

chapter: planning cycle

This Microsoft Excel spreadsheet is designed as an interactive teaching tool.

It is an example of what a hi-level forecast model may look like and achieve, in terms of forecasting earnings of a business for the balance of a current financial period and five years beyond. This tool works best when data is entered systematically, in the cells from the top of the spreadsheet. As each element is completed, evaluate the effect of the assumptions in the income statement, balance sheet, cash flow and the key ratio reports.

Real learning value is derived when it is used in conjunction with the definitions document.

inventory analysis

chapter: keep score

This Microsoft Excel spreadsheet is designed as an interactive teaching tool.

It analyses the effect of aging inventory in a business. It allows simulation of days inventory to calculate the effect on cash flow and interest costs.

management accounts

chapter: keep in score

This PDF document illustrates a suggested presentation of monthly management accounts. Most modern accounting systems have very powerful report writing features, which allow for flexible reports designs.

This presentation demonstrates how monthly values can be compared, progressively, and how each month and the year-to-date results can be compared to a budget forecasts.

market share calculator

chapter: will it work? business plan

This Microsoft Excel spreadsheet is designed as an interactive teaching tool.

It is designed as a check point to compare forecasted sales against the actual market demographic. The calculator consists of five elements: total market size, primary demographics, secondary demographics, target market and competitors' share. It is designed as a reality check for sales forecasts.

net asset management

chapter: financial viability

This Microsoft Excel spreadsheet is designed as an interactive teaching tool.

It uses high-level trading data to demonstrate how a target return on net assets can be achieved. It teaches the formulae related to return on sales (ROS), asset turn (AT) and return on net assets (ROA) and their inter-relationship.

ors

chapter: employees, planning cycle
This PDF document is a sample of a completed objective record sheet and explanations of each of its elements.

receivables analysis

chapter: keep score
This Microsoft Excel spreadsheet is designed as an interactive teaching tool.

It analyses the effect of aging receivables in a business. It allows simulation of days receivables to calculate the effect on cash flow and interest costs.

valuator

chapter: what now?
This Microsoft Excel spreadsheet is designed as an interactive teaching tool.

It teaches the basics of doing a high-level valuation of a business. It is not a comprehensive evaluation tool, but it does provide five basic measurement criteria for evaluation purposes.

working capital

chapter: financial viability
This Microsoft Excel spreadsheet is designed as an interactive teaching tool.

It uses high-level trading data to teach the formulae related to days inventory, days receivables and days payables. It demonstrates how cash flow is affected by setting realistic targets for each working capital element.

getting to value

publisher
BIZZBEAN SA (Pty) Ltd

www.bizzbean.com
copyright Quentin G McCullough 2018

printer
kindle direct publishing

cover design by Wilmie Pretorius

available in print:
first edition in 2018
ISBN: 978-0-620-78577-8

www.ingramcontent.com/pod-product-compliance
Lightning Source LLC
Chambersburg PA
CBHW022036190326
41520CB00008B/604